THE BIRDING PRO'S
FIELD GUIDES

I0120377

Birds of
New Jersey

Marc Parnell

Naturalist & Traveler Press

To my mother,
For whom this book was originally intended.

May all readers of this field guide
enjoy birding as much as we have together.

Printed in the United States of America
First Printing, 2021

ISBN: 978-1-954228-17-7
Library of Congress Control Number: 2021932344

Naturalist & Traveler Press
Cleveland, Ohio

www.thebirdingpro.com

TABLE OF CONTENTS

Note: All species listings are alphabetized and located in the rear index for quick reference.

HOW TO USE THIS GUIDE

Birding by Comparison

This field guide series introduces a new method to bird identification: the **birding by comparison approach**. The objective of this technique is to empower birders to understand how birds might appear in a foreign environment before they have even observed the species, thus allowing them to more quickly and intelligently respond in the field.

First, close your eyes and imagine the size and silhouette of a well-known suburban species, such as the Northern Cardinal. Consider (from memory) how it perches on a branch or birdbath, how large it seems compared to the nearby leaves and vegetation, and how it appears from farther away—such as from across the street.

Now, consider the similarly sized Gray Catbird, a common bird of thickets and wooded edges. While less frequently observed by suburbanites, most nature walks in the warmer months will turn up at least several loudly *mewing* individuals. With eyes closed, superimpose the silhouette of a gray Northern Cardinal into a dense thicket, with the tail visible from one gap in the leaves and the head visible in another. Finally, consider the detailed images and behavior accounts given on the Gray Catbird species page, and modify the mental imagery accordingly.

Such visualization techniques allow the birder to transform each species into a three-dimensional, breathing creature that is practically waiting to jump from the pages. In addition, they prepare the birder in advance for how to locate and identify these birds in a simple, memorable way.

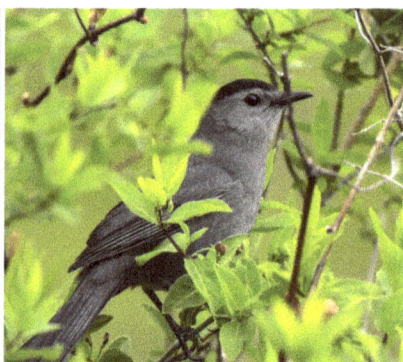

Male Northern Cardinal at left, Adult Gray Catbird at right.
(Note: Both the Gray Catbird and Northern Cardinal are
listed in this guide as measuring 8 ¾ in. from bill to tail.)

Locating Birds in This Guide

When sequentially flipping through the pages of this field guide, you will be viewing all common birds of the region *from largest to smallest*. Once a species in question has been narrowed to a selection of pages, the large images on the left side allow for an easy and painless identification.

In addition, consider the following reference sizes, which may prove helpful when starting out:

- **Very, Very Large**: Great Blue Heron (45 in.), Canada Goose (37 in.), Turkey Vulture (28 in.)
- **Very Large**: Mallard (23 in.), Red-tailed Hawk (22 in.), Ring-billed Gull (19 in.), American Crow (19 in.)
- **Large**: Cooper's Hawk (16 in.), Rock Pigeon/Dove (13 in.), Common Grackle (12 in.)
- **Medium-Large**: Mourning Dove (12 in.), Blue Jay (11 in.), American Robin (10 in.), Northern Cardinal (8 ¾ in.)
- **Medium**: European Starling (8 ¼ in.), Red-winged Blackbird (8 in.), Brown-headed Cowbird (7 ½ in.)
- **Small-Medium**: Downy Woodpecker (6 ¼ in.), Song Sparrow (5 ¾ in.), House Finch (5 ½ in.)
- **Small**: Chipping Sparrow (5 ½ in.), White-breasted Nuthatch (5 ¼ in.), Carolina Wren (5 ¼ in.)
- **Very Small**: American Goldfinch (5 in.), Common Yellowthroat (4 ¾ in.), Ruby-throated Hummingbird (3 ¼ in.)

All species are also listed in the rear index, which provides a complete listing of the birds covered in this field guide.

Understanding Species Listings

Each listing contains detailed information on many aspects of the species' life, sorted into a series of straightforward sections. For more detailed explanations of the written sections, consider the diagrams on the following two pages.

In addition, each species features a full page of color photographs. These have been carefully selected to highlight each species' most significant features and field marks, as well as accurately present the bird in its typical habitat. This should provide a baseline reference when first studying a particular bird, and will thus closely correspond with many field observations.

Frequency Rating: This provides a one to five rating of how likely an average birder is to see the species in a given year. Novices should mostly focus on three- to five-rated birds, while advanced birders will likely be familiar with birds of all ratings.

Common Name: This is the name most often used when describing the species.

Habitat: Describes where the species is most likely to be observed in the wild.

Wild Diet: Describes the food sources most often taken by this species (feeder diet is covered separately in *Bird Feeding Tips*, if applicable).

Migrate: This explains if, or the extent to which, a species migrates in this region.

Eggs: Describes the color, markings, length, and number of eggs. Also, lists the number of broods if greater than one.

Compare to Similar Species: Describes the significant field marks for distinguishing this bird from similar species.

Species Map: Dark-highlighted states indicate the species' presence in the state, while lighter states (of which there are none for the Mourning Dove, a widely common bird) indicate the species' relative absence from the state.

MEDIUM TO LARGE

⑤ **MOURNING DOVE.** *Ze*

SIZE: 12 in.
HABITAT: Open woods, fields, suburbs, roz
WILD DIET: Various seeds.
BEHAVIOR: Often observed perching on repeatedly *hooing* with its signature, meland is not an overly picky eater. To accompany it swallows fine rocks or sands to aid in digesti itself on the ground, with wings and tail spla
MIGRATE? Partially.
NESTING: Hidden among tree branches, objects such as eaves and gutters. Cup-shap grasses, and small sticks. About 8 in. across.
EGGS: White. Length of 1 in. Total of 2. Us raise up to 6.

BIRD FEED:

FEEDER DIET: Black-oil and hulled sunflowe hearts, millet, oats, nyjer, milo. **FEEDER TYI**
BEHAVIOR: May rest or forage beneath feede Hawks, and sometimes Sharp-shinned or even R

COMPARE TO SIMILAR SPECIES: M found in less urban areas. Tapered, feathered which are very different from the more rect American Kestrels, not to mention many oth

DID YOU KNOW? Occasionally called turt in flight—reaching speeds of up to 55 mph as

J   F

BIRDS (8 ½ – 12")

naida macroura.

Size: Indicates the average length from bill to tail.

dsides.

wires, fences, roofs, and in trees, while
oly call. Pecks for food on the ground, and
s voracious appetite for seeds, this species
on. Occasionally may be observed sunning
ed out.

in shrubs, on the ground, or in artificial
ed, and constructed with conifer needles,

ally raises 2-3 broods each year, but may

NG TIPS

r seeds, safflower seed, cracked corn, peanut
ES: Ground, platforms, hoppers. **FEEDER**
s. Common prey for feeder-raiding Cooper's
ed-shouldered Hawks.

---

ich paler than Rock Doves, and usually
tails are easily observable when perching,
ngular tails of Sharp-shinned Hawks and
er visual differences.

le doves, these birds are anything but slow
they whistle through the air.

M A M J J A S O N D

Size Category: Provides a convenient, color-coded indicator of bird size. Eight different sizes are used throughout this book, all of which are listed (with examples) on Page 5.

Scientific Name: This is the name most often used in academic literature.

Behavior: This section provides an extended, in-depth description of how the species spends its days (e.g., foraging, flocking, aggression, flying style, songs and calls, etc.).

Nesting: Describes the location, construction, and size of this species' typical nests.

Bird Feeding Tips: For birds that visit feeders, this section describes which types of food are consumed, which feeders are preferred, and a brief description of behavior.

Did You Know: Provides an interesting fun fact for each species, and often much more.

Monthly Birding Forecast: Provides a simplified chart to show when the species is most observable locally. This forecast allows for birders to selectively target certain species by time of year.

INTRODUCTION TO BIRDING AND BIRD FEEDING

BIRDING

Gear Basics

First on any new birder's wish list must be a pair of suitable binoculars. These can be advertised with a dizzying array of specifications and features.

As far as lenses and magnification are concerned, an 8x42 pair is normally best for beginners and intermediates. The first number refers to the magnification (e.g., 8), which should not exceed 10, and is ideally 7 or 8; the second number refers to the size of the objective lens (e.g., 42 mm), with smaller sizes decreasing overall brightness and field of view. If binoculars with too high of magnification are used, the effective field of view is decreased to the point that quickly locating birds can be extremely difficult.

A good pair of binoculars should cost at least $75, but no more than $300. There are many well-reviewed bins that fall squarely within this price range. However, advanced or professional birders may use binoculars which cost up to $2,500. Keep in mind that increases in cost are often accompanied by marginal benefits, and that an inexpensive pair of binoculars can provide nearly all of the same thrills for a lower entry price, especially for novice or occasional birders.

A mobile application with bird sounds is the next logical item for most birders, and several free options are widely available from most app stores.

This field guide does not include written descriptions of bird calls and songs for every species—though many are included—as it can often be difficult to fully appreciate or even understand songs in this format. Consider downloading the free Audubon (by the National Audubon Society) or Merlin (by the Cornell Lab of Ornithology) mobile apps, which provide audio tracks for each species in a given locality. In addition, some apps even identify birds by their calls in real time, but results can be inconsistent and often require prior expertise on the part of the birder.

A few optional extras must also be mentioned. Many cameras, particularly high-zoom bridge models, are now offering optical zooms in excess of 50x for prices less than $300, which likely proves the most logical starting price point. Spotting scopes are land-based, tripod-mounted telescopes specialized for observing wildlife from a distance, and particularly suited for locating distant shorebirds and waterfowl; many of these scopes can offer up to 60x optical zoom, though quality models often begin near $1,000. Finally, for longer hikes, consider purchasing a bottle of high-SPF sunscreen, a high-capacity water bottle, a first-aid kit, and wading boots (for submerged trails).

Approaching and Identifying Birds in the Field

Keep a safe distance from birds, and be wary of making any sudden movements or noises. Many species are extremely wary of humans, and can vanish into a thicket or behind a tree before the birder is even aware of their presence. (It must also be noted that actively interfering with a bird's ability to forage or nest can affect their chances of long-term survival.) Finally, only explore birding patches on public land, and do not trespass on private property without prior permission—even if there might be a life-list bird lurking in the shadows!

When identifying birds in the field, a stepwise process is often very useful, both for remembering information and prioritizing identification steps. Consider the following:

- First, consider the behavior and habitat of the bird. Is it wading in the shallows of a marsh, like a heron, or perching on the shingles of a house, like a dove?
- Estimate the size of the bird relative to that of others you have observed. For instance, is the bird approximately sparrow-sized, cardinal-sized, duck-sized, etc.?
- Determine the color and primary field marks of the bird in question. If the bird is red, medium-sized, and perched in a tree, does it have a crest like a male Northern Cardinal or black wings like a male Scarlet Tanager?
- Continue to observe the bird while considering these criteria, if possible. Viewing a bird from multiple angles, listening to its vocalizations, and observing its general behavior can further elucidate any puzzling identification challenge.

Finally, consider seeking out local Audubon societies or birding clubs. Partnering with a more experienced companion in the field is one of the best ways to double-check observations and learn more specific or situational techniques. In addition, many of these local organizations sponsor conservation and awareness efforts which are critical for the maintenance of nature for future generations.

BIRD FEEDING

Selecting Feeders

The first feeder selected should be a large, squirrel-proof tube or hopper. These are particularly easy to monitor and refill, and can be filled with a high-quality variety mix or with black-oil sunflower seeds.

For a second feeder, consider mounting suet cages on trees throughout the yard. These can be found in standardized sizes, which fit a wide variety of third-party suet cakes. More hands-on birders might also consider applying the suet directly to the tree bark: most suet cakes easily rub onto the trunk, and provide a more accessible food source for many avian visitors.

The majority of feeder setups would also benefit from a large platform, which can be hung from tree branches or fastened atop a tall, metal pole. Platforms best suit ground-feeding birds, as well as many other species which may be too large to comfortably perch at a tube or hopper feeder. The platform is best filled with a variety mix or black-oil sunflower seed offering.

As a bonus feeder, consider spreading excess seed on the ground nearby, for ground-feeding birds (e.g., doves, sparrows) and mammals (e.g., squirrels, chipmunks). This can often be the most cost-effective way to attract the most species to the backyard, though the ground must be occasionally raked to rid the area of built-up droppings or decomposing feed.

After this point, platform cups with dried mealworms, fresh fruit (e.g., oranges, grapes, or apples), or very small amounts of grape jelly can be added, as well as dedicated hummingbird feeders, hanging seed bells, ground-feeding trays, and hanging thistle tubes for finches. Careful experimentation is often a central tenet of successful bird feeding.

Squirrel-Proofing Feeders

Squirrels are immensely resourceful creatures, and are unlikely to turn down an easy meal—particularly at dedicated feeding stations, which present an enticing opportunity. To ensure that bird feeders serve their originally intended purpose (i.e., feeding the birds), consider the following potential solutions:

- Situate each feeder at least 7-8 ft. away from all nearby trees and branches
- Utilize a tall, metal pole, measuring approximately 5 ft. from the ground to the base of the feeder
- Hang feeders from a line laterally fastened to multiple trees (i.e., the clothesline method)

- Set up a dedicated ground-feeding station to divert squirrels' attention, with a platform or section of ground amply stocked with black-oil sunflower seeds and/or peanuts

Try to refrain from using cayenne pepper, or products which incorporate this spice. While partially effective in discouraging squirrels from consuming the feed (birds have far less sensitive taste buds than mammals), this can be dangerous for the squirrels; if the squirrel touches its eyes after feeding, it may attempt to desperately claw out the foreign particles, leading to partial or full blindness.

Situating Feeders

Bird feeders should be at least 8-12 in. apart from one another, providing ample room for birds to access all openings and perches, as well as reducing the stress imposed on birds when feeding in excessively close quarters.

Additionally, it must be noted that hundreds of millions of birds die each year due to window strikes. As such, best practice for situating feeders is as follows: either 25 feet or more from all nearby windows, or immediately next to any windows. The primary concern with feeders situated in the danger zone—about three to 25 feet away from windows—is that birds can generate enough momentum to make a window strike fatal, while not having sufficient time to avoid the obstacle if quickly fleeing the feeder station (e.g., from a predator, or to seek shelter).

In conclusion, situate feeders as close as possible to low shrubs and/or groves of trees: birds feel more safe with lots of nearby shelter. A metal pole can be used to support a large platform, which is often most effective for attracting the widest variety of birds. All remaining feeders should be squirrel-proofed (e.g., weight-sensitive openings, cages with small openings, or thistle mesh tubes), if possible.

Maintaining Feeders

Bird feed must be replaced at least once a week, particularly in hot or rainy weather, when mold and bacteria growth can be most pernicious. In the special case of hummingbird feeders, each feeder should be completely emptied and refilled at least once every five days, and every two days in warmer weather. Otherwise, the sugar water mixture can ferment, producing toxic levels of alcohol.

THE BIRDING PRO TIP

Sugar water for hummingbirds can be made at home with a four-parts water, one-part white sugar recipe. The water must be brought to a boil before adding sugar, thoroughly stirred, and then allowed to cool afterwards.

Each bird feeder should also be taken down at least once each month for cleaning. The following, stepwise process provides a quick guide to this simple process:

- First, empty all seed.
- Second, scrub away any debris or bird droppings.
- Third, soak the feeder in a weak cleaning solution (e.g., one-part bleach to 10-parts warm water), and gently scrub with a towel.
- Finally, once completely dried (to avoid the growth of mold), the feeder can be refilled and rehung.

If feeders are not regularly cleaned, contagious diseases can quickly spread among local flocks. A commonly observed disease, bacterial conjunctivitis, is common in eastern House Finches; first observed in the 1990s, this causes avian pink eye and eventually leads to full blindness, which itself results in starvation or premature predation.

Nest Boxes and Birdbaths

When considering nest boxes, first ensure that the box in question is made of wood, rather than plastic. Furthermore, individual species often require specific sizes and designs of nest boxes. If you seek to target certain birds, consider searching online for blueprints or for well-reviewed nest boxes listed for sale. Many commercially available, decorative birdhouses fail to successfully attract breeding pairs of birds.

On another note, birdbaths tend to be a fantastic way to attract birds to any backyard. Maximum depths of ¾ to 2 ¼ in. are preferable, with shallower areas near the edges of the basin. A central bubbling feature, if present, helps to prevent insects from settling and congregating around the bath.

Birdbaths must be cleaned two to three times each week. Each basin must be completely emptied, scrubbed clean, soaked in a 1:10 bleach-to-water solution, and thoroughly rinsed before being refilled. If these tasks are not completed, the birdbath can become a breeding ground for various avian diseases—defeating the original purpose of supporting local bird life.

Additional Notes

Plant as much *native* vegetation as possible, and consider leaving brush piles for birds—and other animals—to use as a source of shelter. These simple steps can drastically increase both the diversity and concentration of wildlife in the backyard.

Furthermore, if Black Bears are locally common, consider only setting out feeders in winter (i.e., when bears are hibernating). Otherwise, bears can prove to be a very dangerous nuisance: knocking down and destroying feeders, curiously investigating other parts of the backyard, and even approaching the house. Throughout the remainder of the year, use dense plantings of native shrubs and trees, as well as birdbaths and nest boxes, to safely attract avian visitors.

COLLECTED LIST OF FAQs

BEHAVIOR

Q: *Where do birds go to sleep?*

A: First of all, one common misconception must be addressed: birds do not sleep in nests, with the exception of actively incubating females. Instead, birds sleep—or roost—in a variety of other secure locations.

Waterfowl tend to sleep directly on the water, or on protected shorelines (i.e., with plenty of brush, or on islands). Often present in large flocks, ripples on the water's surface can alert the individuals to any approaching threat. Interestingly, standing waterfowl tend to favor a one-legged stance at their roosts, with the other leg tucked into the belly feathers for warmth.

Large wading birds, such as herons and egrets, tend to roost in the shallows or low in trees, depending on the species. Like many species of waterfowl, wading birds are known to frequently sleep on one leg.

Woodpeckers and nuthatches often roost in cavities, such as natural tree hollows or artificial substitutes. Some birds which nest in cavities, such as wrens, chickadees, and bluebirds, may retire to separate cavity roosts as well.

Crows, starlings, and swallows roost communally. It may be quite common for observers to notice several hundred crows or starlings settling in a grove of trees just before dusk, depending on the location. This strength-in-numbers approach increases safety by application of a collective effort to surveil for predators.

Diurnal birds of prey, such as hawks, may sleep on exposed perches (e.g., telephone poles) or tree branches. In colder weather, individuals are more likely to roost closer to the trunks of mature trees, which slowly dissipate daytime warmth throughout the night.

Finally, most other passerines (i.e., perching birds) tend to roost on sheltered perches in densely vegetated trees, bushes, thickets, and brush piles, often depending on their most frequent daytime haunts. If a predator attempts to climb tree trunks in search of a hasty meal, subtle vibrations are transmitted up the tree and warn any roosting birds of the threat. Like other birds, passerines are more likely to roost closer to the tree trunk during colder bouts of weather.

Q: *Do birds mate for life, or do they change mates throughout a single season?*

A: The vast majority of birds form a moderately stable pair bond for the breeding season, though there may be varying degrees of promiscuity (or "cheating"). However, the pair typically separates by the end of the summer, selecting new mates the following spring. Fewer than one-tenth of all birds exhibit non-monogamous behavior over a single breeding season, with the following patterns occasionally being observed: polygyny, wherein the male takes and protects multiple female mates (e.g., Red-winged Blackbirds); polyandry, where each female has multiple male mates (e.g., Spotted Sandpipers); and full promiscuity, where a less discernible, transient relationship between each "pair" is observed (e.g., some hummingbirds).

Q: *How smart are birds, really? And isn't the expression "bird-brain" used for a good reason?*

A: Birds are fantastically intelligent. Many corvids (e.g., ravens, crows, and jays) possess advanced problem-solving and communicational abilities surpassing those of even domestic dogs and cats, and numerous other species have been proven to have phenomenal long-term memories and multitasking abilities. Among the smartest families of birds are the parrots and the corvids.

Q: *Why don't birds sing as much in the wintertime?*

A: For many birds, the primary purposes of singing include courtship and territorial defense. However, the breeding season only extends from spring through late summer; additionally, many birds may flock together in winter to cooperatively search for scarce food sources, or even disperse over wider, undefended areas. Consequently, some species may lose the ability to sing during these colder months, while others are simply more judicious with the use of their voices.

Q: *When do birds migrate, and how long does it take?*

A: Most birds migrate north between March and May, and migrate south between late August and early October: with more senior individuals making these trips first. It may take some species up to two months to complete their journeys, while shorter-distance migrants may take less than a month. In addition, many birds (with a few exceptions, such as hawks, which soar on warm-air currents by day) take migration flights by night, touching down in a nearby, suitable habitat upon daybreak—analogous to a hungry, road-tripping family seeking out the first available rest stop with several restaurants on hand.

Q: *Do migrating birds return to the same backyard feeders each spring and summer?*

A: Many migratory birds display a certain degree of fidelity to their previous nesting or breeding sites. When coupled with their prodigious navigational faculties, it is entirely plausible (and in many cases, likely) that the very birds observed a year ago are again present in the same local backyard or park.

Q: *Why is migration season the best time to see a wide variety of species, and what is migratory fallout?*

A: Many species do not breed or winter locally, with this region instead serving as a waypoint during spring and/or fall migration. This means that many birds are only observable during certain, migratory months.

Migratory fallout is an event where a large accumulation of birds is observable in a local habitat, often lasting for a few days after a significant weather event. Birds tend to migrate most successfully in the presence of a moderately strong tailwind, with an extended wind of 10-20 mph often serving as the sweet spot. If a favorable wind encourages an above-average number of birds to migrate, and is suddenly interrupted by a major storm, birds will return to ground as soon as possible. With many migrants most active by night, this may lead to a host of activity the following morning—with birds seemingly dripping from every tree branch in sight.

Q: *How do birds survive harsh, northern winters?*

A: Northern-wintering birds have adapted in a variety of ways to survive cold temperatures. Many individuals puff out their feathers and maintain larger fat reserves in an effort to retain more heat, reduce blood flow to the legs to keep their core temperature stable, engage in flocking behavior by day in an effort to locate resources, and some may even roost communally to survive the most frigid of nights.

Q: *Do birds chew their food?*

A: Birds lack teeth, and therefore do not chew in the most conventional sense. Some seed-cracking birds, such as finches, are able to break apart seeds and nuts and eat them in pieces, while raptors are known for tearing apart a fresh kill with their sharp bills. However, large pieces of food are still swallowed, and must be adequately digested.

The solution for birds is a two-stage stomach: with the *gizzard* serving as a second stomach, behind a conventional stomach somewhat resembling that found in many mammals. In species which consume coarser plant materials (e.g., acorns) or hard-shelled invertebrates (e.g., mussels), the gizzard is thick-walled and holds grit and pebbles (which the bird regularly consumes as part of its diet), with the gizzard crushing the mixture to break down otherwise indigestible materials. If present, any harder materials—such as bone, fur, shells, insect exoskeletons, and seed pits—are coalesced into a collected mass, which is coughed up as a *pellet* at a later time. This latter mechanism is most commonly used by larger birds, such as raptors and gulls.

Q: *How do birds bathe?*

A: Birds like to stay clean, too. In areas with sufficient rainfall, individuals commonly bathe by splashing and briefly dunking their heads in puddles and the shallows of ponds, while species in drier climates may give themselves dust baths. These behaviors likely help with feather maintenance. In addition, birds are known to frequently preen themselves throughout the day, with the bill being used to smooth out the feathers and remove small insects.

CONSERVATION

Q: *What is the state of bird conservation efforts today, and are populations decreasing?*

A: Bird conservation may be as organized today as it ever has been, but many global bird populations are still facing an existential threat to their long-term survival. A widely cited, recent study in *Science* found that a staggering three billion birds have been lost from the North American continent over the past 50 years—an overall decline of about 30%. Major threats to avian populations include outdoor housecats (which collectively kill nearly three billion birds in the U.S. and Canada each *year*), habitat loss and redevelopment, pollution, and the use of pesticides and herbicides.

Q: *Have any North American bird species ever been declared extinct?*

A: Unfortunately, yes. In addition to a number of notable subspecies, there are seven species which have been declared extinct in North America over the past 200 years. These include the following, ordered from least to most recent:

- *Great Auk*, a species of coastal water-bird native to the North Atlantic, which likely reached depths of over 250 ft. while diving and measured over 30 in. Some early reports described this bird as the "Northern Penguin," though it was not technically related to the penguins of the Southern Hemisphere. Last confirmed near Iceland, in 1844.

- *Labrador Duck*, a diving duck of the coastal North Atlantic from northeastern Canada to Maryland, which measured about 20 in. Likely uncommon before European colonization. Last confirmed in New York, in 1878.

- *Passenger Pigeon*, a flocking dove of the eastern U.S., which measured about 16 in. Perhaps the most numerous bird in recorded history, with individual flocks reliably estimated at over two billion individuals apiece, and dense nesting colonies covering up to 100 sq. miles. Last confirmed in Indiana, in 1902.

- *Carolina Parakeet*, the only resident North American species of parrot, which ranged throughout the eastern U.S. as far north as New York, and measured about 13 in. This species was hunted as an agricultural pest, a practice which was highly successful due to the parakeets' tendency to return to the fallen members of their flock—perhaps an instinct honed in an effort to collectively swarm predators. Last confirmed in 1904 in Florida, but additional sightings probable through the late 1930s.

- *Ivory-Billed Woodpecker*, a woodpecker larger than the Pileated, which was native to mature, often flooded forests of the Deep South and Cuba and measured about 20 in. This species has been the subject of intensive searches in recent decades, with several unconfirmed reports from the mature, forested swamplands of Louisiana, Arkansas, and Florida. Last confirmed in Louisiana in 1944, and in montane Cuba in 1987.

- *Eskimo Curlew*, a shorebird of the northern tundra which migrated through the Great Plains, measuring about 12 in. May have been among the most numerous North American shorebirds at one point, but was hunted indiscriminately for meat in the late 1800s. Some unconfirmed reports in the last several decades, but last confirmed in Texas in 1962, or in Nebraska in 1987.

- *Bachman's Warbler*, a yellow and gray warbler which bred in flooded forests of the southeastern U.S., and measured about 4 1/4 in. A habitually early migrant, most individuals are thought to have wintered in Cuba. Last confirmed in Louisiana, in 1988.

Q: *How have changing habitats due to human development affected birds?*

A: With many birds specially adapted for specific ecological niches, the influence of human development has resulted in a set of wide-ranging effects. A few key examples of this are as follows.

Brown-headed Cowbirds, formerly limited to the Great Plains, have been able to move into much of the eastern United States; the fragmentation of wooded habitats for new suburban developments has created vast swaths of fringe habitat perfectly suited for the cowbirds. This species widely practices brood parasitism during the breeding season, wherein the female lays her eggs in a variety of other songbirds' nests, who in turn rear the foreign young. While a natural fixture of its former haunts, this parasitic trait has threatened many species of forest-dwelling sparrows and warblers in its newly acquired ranges.

On the other hand, while much of New England was used for agriculture in the early years of colonization, large tracts of land began to gradually rewild circa 1900 as urban centers began to consolidate around heavy industry. This led to the loss of many grassland and open-habitat species from these areas, such as the Barn Owl and the Bobolink (as well as diminishing populations of the Brown-headed Cowbird), which returned to their former, more westerly ranges—a shift which perfectly illustrates many species' opportunism in embracing new geographies, so long as they match certain habitat criteria.

The practice of replanting forests after they have been logged is laden with additional complications. Many of these replanted forests consist of very few tree species, all of which are fast-growing and planted in such a way to reduce subsequent forest fires. However, birds and other animals require a natural diversity of woodland flora, and many other species specialize in transitional woodland (i.e., rewilding habitat full of thickets and saplings). Fires and seemingly unsightly thickets are, in fact, quite normal—therefore, letting nature take its original course is usually the best practice.

It must also be noted that grassland birds, which predominantly inhabit the Great Plains and Midwest, have suffered far greater declines in the past 100 years than many other types of species. This is largely due to the mass cultivation of arable land for agriculture. Unfettered grasslands have been lost at a historic pace, though this has not been discussed as widely: perhaps due to the subtler visual changes to the landscape.

Q: *What are the effects of global warming on the avian world, and what should be expected in the coming decades?*

A: On average, bird populations have been inching northward in past years, with many species moving approximately 10 to 15 miles north per decade. The multifactorial changes to habitat associated with global warming (e.g., melting permafrost, increased forest fires, drying river beds) are likely to only worsen the issue of declining bird populations in future years.

Q: *What are the effects of pesticides?*

A: Pesticides have been one of the primary causes of the precipitous insect declines of the past several decades. Estimates are wide-ranging, but it presently seems that insect populations have decreased by about 40% in the past 50 years. A startling example of this trend is found in the decline of the once-abundant Monarch Butterfly, with populations of this species having declined by well over three-quarters in the past several decades. Collectively, these events have critical trickle-down effects throughout the ecosystem, and are likely a driving factor behind other animal diversity crises.

Q: *How do large glass surfaces and nighttime lighting affect migrating birds?*

A: Lights tend to attract birds, particularly during nocturnal migration flights. This, in combination with the large glass windows which tend to accompany nighttime lighting in urban areas, has led to masses of stunned and deceased birds falling to the pavement in cities all throughout North America. As many as one billion birds die each year in the U.S. due to window strikes of this nature. To combat this issue, many cities have recently launched campaigns to introduce bird-friendly windows and auto-off lighting in tall office buildings.

IDENTIFICATION

Q: *I saw a fully or partially white bird at my feeders. What are leucism, albinism, and melanism?*

A: Both leucism and albinism can result in the manifestation of unusual whiteness. Leucism results in partial pigmentation, with some feathers developing normally and others becoming a patchy white. This is far more common than albinism, which is a rare condition in which all feathers are white and the eyes are a washed-out pink; this is due to a complete inability to produce pigmentation.

Leucistic female Boat-tailed Grackle pictured above.
Note that a normal individual would be fully brown and black.

Melanism, on the other hand, involves overactive pigment production, wherein the bird has a visibly darker (or even blackish) appearance. This condition is likely rarer than both leucism and albinism.

White-winged Dove exhibiting melanism above. Note that this species is normally a pale taupe (i.e., similar to Mourning Dove), rather than brown as pictured.

In addition, the exceptionally rare case of xanthochroism, or xanthism, results in excessively yellow individuals. This is normally due to a genetic condition, but could theoretically be rooted in dietary causes as well.

Q: *How often do birds molt their feathers?*

A: Most birds molt their flight feathers—or *remiges*—once each year, and molt their body feathers one or two times per year.

Q: *What are breeding and nonbreeding plumages, and for which months does each term apply?*

A: Breeding plumage is often displayed by adults from April until August; this plumage demonstrates the health or virility of potential mates, and may be incorporated into some courtship rituals. Nonbreeding plumage, on the other hand, is usually displayed from August through March. The nonbreeding plumage is normally duller, so as to reduce visibility from potential predators throughout the remainder of the year.

BACKYARDS AND BIRD FEEDERS

Q: *What should I do with an injured bird?*

A: If an injured bird is located, particularly in the backyard, it is normally best to leave it alone for a short period. However, if the individual is alive but remains immobilized, a conscientious birder should locate and contact a local wildlife rehabilitation clinic for further instructions.

Q: *How have bird feeders contributed to the size and distribution of bird populations?*

A: Casually scattering seeds on the ground for birds has been practiced since the first millennium, A.D., but dedicated bird feeders only came on the scene in the early 1900s, with widespread adoption picking up in the middle decades of the 20th Century. Some species which were previously observed at more southerly latitudes, such as the Northern Cardinal and Tufted Titmouse, are common today throughout the Great Lakes and Northeast, while Mourning Doves now stay the winter across both of these regions. Many other populations of native, feeder-visiting species have been bolstered by this rising tide as well. However, feeders are widely blamed for accelerating the spread of the House Finch throughout the eastern U.S., in addition to abetting the localized explosions of invasive House Sparrow populations. In short, feeders have dramatically impacted the avian landscape, but in more good ways than bad.

Q: *Which birds are more likely to push around others at a contested feeder?*

A: In general, larger birds tend to best assert their dominance when visiting crowded feeders. However, woodpeckers tend to frequently displace larger birds, and House Finches often outcompete slightly larger Purple Finches.

Note: For additional information on this subtopic, please see the previous section, entitled "Introduction to Birding and Bird Feeding."

THE
BIRDS

② **MUTE SWAN.** *Cygnus olor.*

SIZE: 59 in.

HABITAT: Lakes, ponds, large rivers, harbors, coastlines. May visit urban areas.

WILD DIET: Mostly aquatic vegetation, also supplemented by small animals, insects.

BEHAVIOR: Highly adaptable, this non-native species from Europe is a voracious forager and selects any habitat with sufficient vegetation for feeding. In habitats with plentiful aquatic vegetation, a single Mute Swan may consume as much as 10 pounds of plant matter each day, while uprooting even more—in most cases, outstripping the rate of regrowth. Known to occasionally drift around a section of water with its wings held slightly back, as if sailing. In addition, may be very aggressive during breeding season, with individuals known to attack animals, humans, and even small boats.

MIGRATE? No.

NESTING: Selects a slightly elevated location near shore. A mound of vegetation is constructed from nearby vegetation, upon which a small bowl is carved. Often reused from year to year. About 4 ½ ft. across and 2 ft. deep.

EGGS: Chalky gray to light blue-green. Length of 4 in. Total of 3-8.

FEEDER BEHAVIOR: Does not visit feeders.

COMPARE TO SIMILAR SPECIES: Orange bill among adults is distinctive. Bill position on head is often slightly lower compared to other swan species.

DID YOU KNOW? Mute Swan numbers in North America have more than quintupled in some areas since the year 2000. Their habit of chasing off other species and destructively consuming large amounts of vegetation have threatened the populations of other native species, such as dabbling ducks, geese, and native swans. In addition, the reduction in vegetation at some sites has threatened fish nurseries, which consequently has trickle-up effects throughout the food chain.

J F M A M J J A S O N D

Adult with juvenile at top,
Adult at bottom.

Adult at top (Photo by Dominic Sherony / CC BY-SA / Cropped),
Adults in flight at bottom.

① **TUNDRA SWAN.** *Cygnus columbianus*.

SIZE: 52 in.

HABITAT: Lakes, bays, ponds, large rivers, and coastlines. May visit agricultural (especially, grain) fields during winter.

WILD DIET: Mostly aquatic vegetation. During winter, leftover grains and crops as well.

BEHAVIOR: Often floating in the shallows of medium to large bodies of water. To access food sources, individuals periodically upend themselves to dip their heads below water. While these birds breed near the Arctic, they migrate through sections of North America to access their wintering grounds, usually along oceanic coastlines. During fall and winter, often found in large, noisy flocks—these may be seen overhead in flight, with long, conspicuously extended necks pointing toward the eventual destination.

MIGRATE? Yes.

NESTING: Selects a slightly elevated location near wetlands. Cup-shaped bowl, constructed of various strands of loose vegetation. About 1 ½ ft. across and 6 in. deep.

EGGS: White. Length of 4 in. Total of 3-6.

FEEDER BEHAVIOR: Does not visit feeders.

COMPARE TO SIMILAR SPECIES: The larger Trumpeter Swan also has a black bill, but it extends to the eye and culminates in a sharper V-shape; the Tundra instead has a black bill which stops short of the eye in a rounded U-shape, with *a yellow spot in front of the eye*. In addition, the crown of the Trumpeter's head is angular, while the Tundra's crown is comparatively rounded. Adult Mute Swans have orange bills with a black protrusion at the upper edge.

DID YOU KNOW? As is the case with many swans, Tundra Swans are somewhat unique in that they monogamously mate for life, and may even remain single for the remainder of their lives should one mate die before the other.

| J | F | M | A | M | J | J | A | S | O | N | D |

VERY, VERY LARGE BIRDS (24" AND LARGER)

③ **GREAT BLUE HERON.** *Ardea herodias.*

SIZE: 45 in.

HABITAT: Coastlines, wetlands, rivers, sometimes fields.

WILD DIET: Primarily fish, though various aquatic wildlife—as well as small mammals and ducklings—may sometimes be taken.

BEHAVIOR: Often observed standing motionless at the edge of bodies of water, waiting for prey. When a nearby fish is spotted, the heron normally strikes from a standing position; however, individuals sometimes chase after their quarry by briskly walking through the water, with head cocked. These birds are usually only seen by suburbanites as they fly from one feeding location to another, though they are among the most common and easily observable wetland birds of this region. Flying motion is languid and wingbeats are somewhat labored, with long legs extended behind.

MIGRATE? Partially.

NESTING: Typically nests in groups (known as heronries) in remote areas, particularly in and atop trees, though some may build nests in safe locations at ground level. Sticks and vegetative debris are used to build a bulky platform. About 2-4 ft. across, and up to 2 ft. thick.

EGGS: Light blue. Length of 2 ½ - 3 in. Total of 3-5.

FEEDER BEHAVIOR: Does not visit feeders.

COMPARE TO SIMILAR SPECIES: Large size and dull blue-to-gray coloration distinguishes this species from other large wading birds. Trailing legs, as well as slow and direct flight motion, differentiate from Turkey Vulture.

DID YOU KNOW? While the Great Blue Heron primarily hunts in the calm shallows, some regional populations have developed their own unique approaches. For instance, individuals on the west coast of North America have been known to stand atop floating kelp beds while hunting, and some in the southeastern U.S. have even adapted to hunt in intertidal zones amid high, rolling waves.

J F M A M J J A S O N D

Adults at top and bottom.

Male displaying at top (Photo by Vince Pahkala / CC BY-SA / Cropped),
Female with juveniles at bottom (Photo by D. Gordon E. Robertson / CC BY-SA / Cropped).

② WILD TURKEY. *Meleagris gallopavo*.

SIZE: 39 in.

HABITAT: Edges of woods, especially near clearings and fields.

WILD DIET: Nuts, large seeds, berries, insects and spiders, and occasionally small reptiles and amphibians.

BEHAVIOR: Active foragers, typically walking along the ground. To locate the nuts and seeds which it usually takes for food, individuals often scratch away leaf litter from the forest floor in an effort to uncover any unclaimed morsels. These tidbits are stored along with an assortment of gravelly rocks in the turkey's large gizzard, which slowly grinds the plant matter into more readily digestible pieces. In winter, this portly bird—with males weighing in excess of 15 pounds—may even climb into evergreens to search for any unclaimed food sources.

MIGRATE? No.

NESTING: Areas surrounded by thick shrubbery or tree growth are typically chosen, though some individuals have been known to nest in overgrown fields. An inch-deep depression in the soil is scraped away, upon which the female lays and incubates her eggs. About 12-18 in. across.

EGGS: Light yellow or tan, with red and brown flecks. Length of 2 - 2 ½ in. Total of 8-16.

FEEDER BEHAVIOR: Does not visit feeders, but may be attracted to backyards with native nut-bearing or berry vegetation, particularly if there is nearby woodland.

COMPARE TO SIMILAR SPECIES: Distinctive, and unlike many other birds of this region.

DID YOU KNOW? Wild Turkeys lack adequate night vision, and therefore must roost in trees at night to avoid predators. Individuals have been observed as high as 50 feet above the ground, often selecting some of the highest available perches available in a sturdy, older-growth tree.

J   F   M   A   M   J   J   A   S   O   N   D

① **NORTHERN GANNET.** *Morus bassanus*.

SIZE: 39 in.

HABITAT: Saltwater coastlines of the North Atlantic.

WILD DIET: Small schooling fish (e.g., anchovies, sardines) and squid.

BEHAVIOR: The gannet flies at heights of 50 to 200 feet above the water surface, searching for schools of fish below. Once identified, individuals dive at speeds in excess of 50 mph, plunge 30 to 50 feet beneath the surface, and swallow fish whole before resurfacing. The dive is made with wings tucked close against the body, so as to maximize the depth reached; however, some individuals have been known to use their wings to propulsively swim to even greater depths. Foraging may occur over 100 miles from coastlines, with birds known to follow fishing trawlers in hopes of an easy meal. Thousands of individuals nest together in colonies, which are also sometimes known as gannetries.

MIGRATE? Yes.

NESTING: Selects a location on a rocky coastline, and constructs nest from grasses, mud, and seaweed. Nests are in close proximity to those of other gannets. About 1 ft. across.

EGGS: Pale blue or white. Length of 3 in. Total of 1.

FEEDER BEHAVIOR: Does not visit feeders.

COMPARE TO SIMILAR SPECIES: The uncommon Masked Booby is typically found south of the Northern Gannet's range, and has greater portions of black across the wings and tail (while the Northern Gannet just has black on wingtips), as well as a black "mask" over the eyes.

DID YOU KNOW? The North American population of this species nests entirely in just a few large colonies, with each sometimes hosting tens of thousands of individuals. These sites are situated along the coast of southeastern Canada.

J F M A M J J A S O N D

Adult at top left (Photo by Becky Matsubara / CC BY-SA / Cropped),
Subadult at top right (Photo by Stephen Gidley / CC BY-SA / Cropped),
Adult flying at bottom (Photo by Liam Quinn / CC BY-SA).

Adults at top and bottom.

③ GREAT EGRET. *Ardea alba*.

SIZE: 38 in.

HABITAT: Usually wetlands, but also calm rivers, lakes, and ponds.

WILD DIET: Mostly small fish and frogs, but also small mammals, insects, birds, and reptiles.

BEHAVIOR: Often observed standing motionless in the shallows of a pond or marsh, waiting to strike a fish that swims its way. This species' feeding technique is similar to that of the Great Blue Heron, with individuals either standing still in wait, or slowly wading into the fringes of schooling fish; this preambulatory stalking culminates with a sudden strike of the bill into the water, after which the fish is swallowed whole in a series of occasionally cumbersome, stepwise motions. Flies with long, lumbering wingbeats as it moves between feeding locations: one must watch for its cocked neck and long, trailing legs. A rattling, croaking call may also be given during these brief aerial excursions.

MIGRATE? Yes.

NESTING: Nests colonially in trees overlooking wetlands, situated dozens of feet off the ground. Platform is constructed of sticks and lined with grasses. About 2-3 ft. across and 8 in. deep.

EGGS: Pale blue or green. Length of 2 ½ in. Total of 3-5.

FEEDER BEHAVIOR: Does not visit feeders.

COMPARE TO SIMILAR SPECIES: Most similar to Snowy Egrets or juvenile Little Blue Herons, but the larger size of the Great Egret is the best and most obvious differentiator.

DID YOU KNOW? While this species does not naturally occur in Europe, it has been known to occasionally wander east of its normal range. In the past decade alone, breeding pairs of Great Egrets have successfully reproduced and potentially begun to establish themselves in the British Isles and in Scandinavia.

J F M A M J J A S O N D

35

④ CANADA GOOSE. *Branta canadensis*.

SIZE: 37 in.

HABITAT: Shallows of ponds and lakes, wetlands, and large fields.

WILD DIET: Various grasses and grains, occasionally insects and small fish.

BEHAVIOR: Often seen in large flocks, particularly flying overhead in V-formation while insouciantly honking. The V-formation is typically employed to decrease wind resistance while affording each individual a forward view; throughout longer flights, the geese will cycle positions to more equally share the workload. Prefers to graze in large fields and lawns, or while floating in aquatic habitat, often near the shallows. This species has adapted very well to human development, with many individuals no longer migrating to the southern U.S. for the winter, as had always been the case before. Consequently, Canada Geese are now commonly observed in the lawns abutting office parks, near urban ponds, or in a variety of other well-populated areas. However, individuals may be aggressive toward humans if they feel threatened, and it is therefore best to always keep a safe distance.

MIGRATE? Partially.

NESTING: A slightly elevated area is chosen, upon which a shallow, bowl-shaped nest is constructed of loose vegetation and lined with feathers. About 1 ½ - 2 ft. across.

EGGS: Off-white. Length of 3 in. Total of 3-7.

FEEDER BEHAVIOR: Does not visit feeders.

COMPARE TO SIMILAR SPECIES: The far less common Cackling Goose has similar markings, though this species has much shorter necks, stubbier bills, and is closer to 25 in. in length on average.

DID YOU KNOW? Canada Geese are among the most common birds to be struck by aircraft, likely due to their flocking behavior and tendency to feed in large fields. It has been estimated that these birds have caused tens of millions of dollars' worth of damage to aircraft in the United States in the past few decades, though predator decoys and habitat relocation efforts have been moderately effective in recent years.

J F M A M J J A S O N D

Adult at top,
Adult with juveniles, or goslings, at bottom.

Adult at top,
Juvenile at bottom (Photo by KetaDesign / CC BY-SA).

② BALD EAGLE. *Haliaeetus leucocephalus*.

SIZE: 34 in.

HABITAT: Coastlines of various bodies of water (e.g., rivers, lakes, reservoirs, and oceans), particularly with adjacent, mature woods.

WILD DIET: Mostly fish (usually up to 24 in. in size), but also carrion, other birds, and mammals.

BEHAVIOR: Flies with powerful wingbeats, often selecting perches in tall, mature trees. Frequently captures fish by swooping low and reaching its talons just beneath the surface, though some individuals may also harass other predators (e.g., ospreys, gulls, and even otters) to steal a fresh catch. The spectacular courtship displays of this bird are among the most widely discussed in the avian world, with male and female locking talons in midair before tumbling downward together—only separating at the final moment to avoid striking the ground.

MIGRATE? Partially.

NESTING: Often selects mature conifers, with optimal location near the top. Sticks and grasses are used to construct a nest, or eyrie, that may grow to be as large as 8 ft. wide and deep, and over a ton in weight. Breeding pairs typically return to the same nests each year.

EGGS: Various shades of white. Length of 3 in. Total of 2-3.

FEEDER BEHAVIOR: Does not visit feeders.

COMPARE TO SIMILAR SPECIES: Juveniles may be confused with large hawks or Golden Eagles. To distinguish, note the mottled, dirty coloration of feathers and the fingered ends of wings. However, the white markings of adults are very much distinct.

DID YOU KNOW? Though Bald Eagles numbered in the hundreds of thousands as recently as the late 1800s, hunting and DDT pesticide use reduced the total number of nesting pairs in the contiguous U.S. to under 500 by the 1950s. Federal protections have since allowed these populations to recover, with nearly 20,000 nesting pairs in the U.S. today. Furthermore, Bald Eagles are now so numerous in the Aleutian Islands that locals of Dutch Harbor, Alaska have taken to calling them "Dutch Harbor pigeons."

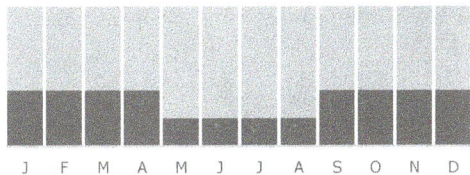

J F M A M J J A S O N D

③ DOUBLE-CRESTED CORMORANT.
Phalacrocorax auritus.

SIZE: 32 in.

HABITAT: Coastlines, harbors, large lakes and rivers. Infrequently found in smaller lakes, ponds, and wetlands.

WILD DIET: Mostly fish (up to 12 in. in size).

BEHAVIOR: Often observed sitting low in the water before swiftly diving to hunt for prey. This species may swim as deep as 50 feet in search of food. Individuals also form large, conspicuous flocks on piers and sandbars as they dry their feathers in the sun. These flocks collectively consume a great quantity of fish, with each cormorant ingurgitating about one pound of food daily; consequently, cormorant populations in the Great Lakes alone take nearly 80 million pounds of fish yearly.

MIGRATE? Partially.

NESTING: Colonial nesters, usually selecting locations in trees or on protected rocky shorelines. Bowl-shaped, and comprised of twigs and feathers. About 2 ft. in diameter and 8 in. high.

EGGS: Off-white, possibly with shades of pale blue. Length of 2 ½ in. Total of 1-6.

FEEDER BEHAVIOR: Does not visit feeders.

COMPARE TO SIMILAR SPECIES: The adult Great Cormorant is slightly larger and stockier through the body, and has a white flank patch and white patch behind the bill; meanwhile, juvenile Greats have mostly white bellies, and juvenile Double-cresteds only have white on the upper chest. The Neotropic Cormorant is much smaller and also has a proportionately smaller head and bill.

DID YOU KNOW? Double-crested Cormorants are not particularly gracious tenants. After several years of reusing nests in a given tree, the excessive guano buildup on the ground beneath will often kill the tree outright, forcing the nesters to move to another nearby site.

J F M A M J J A S O N D

Adult swimming at top,
Adult resting at bottom left (Photo by Frank Schulenberg / CC BY-SA / Cropped),
Juvenile at bottom right (Photo by Virginia State Parks / CC BY-SA / Cropped).

Breeding adults swimming at top,
Nonbreeding adult at bottom.

① COMMON LOON (or GREAT NORTHERN DIVER). *Gavia immer*.

SIZE: 31 in.

HABITAT: Mostly deep, medium- to large-sized lakes, and oceanic coastlines.

WILD DIET: Fish (e.g., bass, sunfish, and walleye).

BEHAVIOR: As with the grebes, this species has legs which are set far behind the body's center of gravity, making for awkward land-based walking but prolific swimming abilities. Individuals have been known to make split-second changes of direction, rapid propulsive movements, and quick gyrations around underwater obstacles in pursuit of prey, which are brought to the surface and engulfed headfirst. Their high degree of wing-loading requires long takeoff areas for flight, thus necessitating larger bodies of water for feeding.

MIGRATE? Yes.

NESTING: Chooses a quiet, sheltered site on the shore, usually on a small island. A mound with an inner bowl is formed from wet vegetative debris, and may reach sizes of up to 2 ft. across.

EGGS: Yellow-brown with dirty blotches. Length of 3 ½ in. Total of 2.

FEEDER BEHAVIOR: Does not visit feeders, but may use nesting platforms.

COMPARE TO SIMILAR SPECIES: Larger than other North American loons, breeding adults have distinct head plumage with a jet-black bill. Nonbreeding adults are well identified from the side, with the demarcation between dark and white coloration along the neck somewhat patchy and irregular (the Pacific Loon has a nearly straight line), though roughly along the median.

DID YOU KNOW? This species is perhaps most famous for its whooping, whistling yodels and wails, which have ethereally drifted over the surfaces of placid lakeshores and coastlines for millennia. It has also featured in many traditions of Native American spiritual folklore, and on the Canadian one-dollar coin.

J F M A M J J A S O N D

① **SNOW GOOSE.** *Anser caerulescens.*

SIZE: 30 in.

HABITAT: Shallows of lakes and ponds, wetlands, and fields. In summer, breeds in the far northern tundra.

WILD DIET: Various aquatic vegetation and agricultural grains. Sometimes, fruits and berries.

BEHAVIOR: Often found loitering or noisily honking in very large flocks, this species forages in the shallows of wetlands or bays, or gleans waste grains from agricultural fields. Though flocks tend to fly at very high altitudes, they may sometimes be observed swirling and settling into a communal roosting location—a truly spectacular sight. At night, individuals may roost floating on the water, sitting, or standing one-legged. Common predators across much of their range include mammals ranging in size from foxes to bears, as well as eagles.

MIGRATE? Yes.

NESTING: Colonial nester. Selects a high-ground location, often near a pond or bog. A shallow nest scrape is lined with grasses and feathers. Up to 3 ft. across.

EGGS: Shades of white, with older eggs more heavily stained. Length of 3 in. Total of 3-6.

FEEDER BEHAVIOR: Does not visit feeders.

COMPARE TO SIMILAR SPECIES: The uncommon Ross's Goose is very similar, with notable differences including the following: the Ross's has a blunter bill with bluish coloring behind the nostrils; lacks a blackish, grin-like opening between the upper and lower bill; and *lacks a distinct curve along the vertical base of the bill.*

DID YOU KNOW? There are actually two color morphs of the Snow Goose: the white Snow, and the much less common Blue. The Blue morph features mostly dark plumage from the lower neck down.

J F M A M J J A S O N D

Snow/white adult at top,
Blue adult at bottom (Photo by Trish Hartmann / CC BY-SA / Cropped).

Adult perching at top (Photo by Devra Cooper / CC BY-SA),
Soaring at bottom.

⑤ TURKEY VULTURE. *Cathartes aura*.

SIZE: 28 in.

HABITAT: Sparse woods, open fields, roadsides, landfills.

WILD DIET: Carrion, human garbage (up to one-quarter of total dietary intake may consist of artificial materials inadvertently consumed at landfills).

BEHAVIOR: Slowly, wobblingly flies and circles above the countryside, with its long, broad wings held in a shallow V-shape. Throughout the day, this species takes advantage of rising currents of warm air, which enable individuals to effortlessly glide along with very few, if any, wingbeats; these currents, known as *thermals*, are also used by other raptors, such as Red-tailed Hawks, as they scan the countryside for food. Once several 50-degree days occur in a row, Turkey Vultures tend to migrate south for the winter, given that the strength of thermal currents proportionately decreases with daytime temperatures. Solitary individuals or small groups may be observed feeding on carrion along abandoned roadsides.

MIGRATE? Partially.

NESTING: Little to no nest construction. Selects rocky openings, such as caves and crevices, as well as hollowed trees and animal burrows.

EGGS: Milky white with irregular red-brown spotting. Length of 3 in. Total of 2.

FEEDER BEHAVIOR: Does not visit feeders, though can be attracted by animal carcasses.

COMPARE TO SIMILAR SPECIES: The Black Vulture lacks the black-and-tan pattern on the underwing, as well as a red head.

DID YOU KNOW? Turkey Vultures are one of the few birds to possess a sense of smell, by which it finds its food sources. Interestingly, natural gas maintenance employees have repeatedly reported Turkey Vultures congregating en masse after pipelines have burst. This is due to the presence of the natural gas additive ethyl mercaptan, which is also released by decaying flesh.

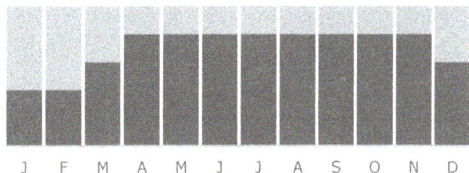

J F M A M J J A S O N D

③ GREAT BLACK-BACKED GULL. *Larus marinus.*

SIZE: 28 in.

HABITAT: Coastlines, often of large bodies of water. Also landfills.

WILD DIET: Mostly fish, but also garbage at landfills, other birds, and aquatic invertebrates.

BEHAVIOR: Active forager at the surface of water and at garbage dumps. Historically limited to the oceanic coastlines of the North Atlantic, droves of Great Black-backed Gulls have been moving inland to the Great Lakes, supported by the usage of garbage dumps as supplementary—or even primary—feeding sites. Often observed milling around large parking lots and piers, particularly in mixed flocks of gulls.

MIGRATE? Partially.

NESTING: Prefers to select islands or other locations less accessible to predators. Vegetation and garbage are often used as nest materials, which are placed atop a raised object, such as a large rock or a tree stump.

EGGS: Tan, brown, or brown-green, with dark speckles. Length of 3 in. Total of 2-3.

FEEDER BEHAVIOR: Does not visit feeders.

COMPARE TO SIMILAR SPECIES: This is the largest of all gull species, and is identifiable by the dark gray-to-black coloration on the upper side of wings. Individuals are best differentiated from the less common Lesser Black-Backed Gull by notable size difference and leg color (the Lesser features bright yellow, rather than dull pink, legs).

DID YOU KNOW? A voracious predator of seemingly anything that will fit in its mouth, the Great Black-Backed Gull is one of the only gull species which actively hunts smaller birds. This behavior is most common throughout the breeding season, when abundant nestlings and fledglings often prove to be an easy meal. However, adults sometimes also pursue seabirds such as puffins, as well as terrestrial songbirds up to 12 inches in length.

J   F   M   A   M   J   J   A   S   O   N   D

Adult loafing at top,
Adult hunting at bottom (fish pictured is a flounder).

Adult perching at top (Photo by Dick Daniels / CC BY-SA),
Adult soaring at bottom.

③ **BLACK VULTURE.** *Coragyps atratus*.

SIZE: 25 in.
HABITAT: Sparse woods, open fields, roadsides, landfills.
WILD DIET: Carrion.
BEHAVIOR: Alternates between short series of quick, forceful wingbeats and gliding. Often gathers in flocks: sometimes resting on roofs, sometimes flying high in the air. While it does not have the same sense of smell as the Turkey Vulture, it resourcefully compensates by watching the activities of its cousins; if it notices scavenging activity, a flock of Black Vultures will quickly overwhelm a feeding Turkey Vulture and assume control of the feeding site. Only the Crested Caracara of southern Texas readily displaces Black Vulture flocks at carcasses.
MIGRATE? No.
NESTING: Cavity nester, selecting locations such as caves, hollows in trees, or spaces in abandoned buildings. Eggs are laid directly on the ground, or floor of cavity.
EGGS: Light tan to light blue-green. Length of 3 in. Total of 2-3.
FEEDER BEHAVIOR: Does not visit feeders, though can be attracted by animal carcasses.

COMPARE TO SIMILAR SPECIES: The more common Turkey Vulture has a black-and-tan pattern on the underwing, a red head, and a visibly longer tail in flight. In addition, if observed closely, the legs of the Black Vulture often extend past the trailing edge of the tail in flight.

DID YOU KNOW? Though New World vultures (such as this species) closely resemble many of the characteristics found in vultures of the Old World, the two groups actually lack a common genetic ancestor. Both lead similar lifestyles, and therefore have adapted convergently: their bald heads are similarly useful in preventing bacterial growth in feathers; pointed, durable beaks allow for efficient tearing of carcasses; and wide wings allow for gliding flights conducive to locating food. Even so, many other behaviors still differ.

J F M A M J J A S O N D

② COMMON MERGANSER. *Mergus merganser.*

SIZE: 25 in.

HABITAT: Lakes, rivers, streams, and ponds, especially if near mature, dense woods.

WILD DIET: Mostly fish, but also aquatic invertebrates, amphibians, and occasionally small mammals or birds.

BEHAVIOR: This species is a diving duck, which means that it fully submerges and swims underwater when in search of prey. It may stay underwater for up to a minute, and grasps its prey with the serrated edges of its bill. Known for organized group hunting as well, whereby the mergansers chase a fish into shallow water for easier capture. Spends most of its time on the water.

MIGRATE? Yes.

NESTING: Cavity nesters, usually selecting a nest near wetlands with an entrance hole at least 6 in. in diameter. May place loose vegetation, feathers on the floor.

EGGS: White or whitish-tan. Length of 2 ½ in. Total of 8-13.

FEEDER BEHAVIOR: Does not visit feeders, but does use nest boxes.

COMPARE TO SIMILAR SPECIES: Red-breasted Merganser also features males with green heads and females with red heads, with similar silhouette. However, male Common Mergansers have a white body (apart from upper back) and lack a reddish breast; meanwhile, male Red-breasteds have brown and white sides, a trailing tuft on the head, and a white stripe on neck with red-brown upper chest. In addition, female Commons have darker head and neck coloration than their Red-breasted counterparts.

DID YOU KNOW? Gulls—and even some raptors—are known to shadow flocks of Common Mergansers in hopes of stealing any captured prey once the ducks surface. This practice is known as *kleptoparasitism*.

J F M A M J J A S O N D

Male at top,
Female at bottom.

Male at top,
Two males with female at bottom.

① NORTHERN PINTAIL. *Anas acuta.*

SIZE: 25 in.

HABITAT: Shallows of open wetlands, flooded fields and marshes, lakes.

WILD DIET: Seeds and roots of aquatic plants, aquatic invertebrates, and terrestrial grains and seeds.

BEHAVIOR: This species is a member of the dabbling ducks, and thus periodically tips forward to feed, submerging its head and neck underwater. It mostly feeds at dusk or nighttime. The Northern Pintail's long neck, especially compared to those of some other dabbling ducks, allows it to reach more than one foot beneath the surface for vegetation. However, pintails are frequently observed in the muddy shallows of ephemeral ponds and puddles, rooting in the substrate for vegetation. Like other waterfowl, this species molts its feathers in late summer and temporarily becomes flightless; in response, most Northern Pintails remain secretive for this period. Individuals may be spotted walking about in agricultural fields or meadows during the winter, searching for grains and seeds.

MIGRATE? Yes.

NESTING: Ground nester, sometimes far from water. Scrapes an impression into the ground, upon which loose, matted grasses are placed. About 9 in. wide and 3 in. deep.

EGGS: Shades of white, possibly with dirty mottling. Length of 2 in. Total of 6-9.

FEEDER BEHAVIOR: Does not visit feeders.

COMPARE TO SIMILAR SPECIES: Male's long tail and distinct head and neck markings allow for a simple identification. Female is often situated near males, but the dark gray bill and brown-and-white feathered sides should be noticed.

DID YOU KNOW? Long-distance migrants, this species can fly for up to 2,000 miles nonstop and at speeds of up to 50 mph: perhaps even faster in the presence of a forceful tailwind. Its breeding grounds range from the Arctic Circle to the northern U.S., and its wintering grounds are as far south as Central America and the Caribbean.

J F M A M J J A S O N D

55

② **SNOWY EGRET.** *Egretta thula.*

SIZE: 24 in.

HABITAT: Mostly wetlands, but also lakes, ponds, and coastlines.

WILD DIET: Small fish, aquatic invertebrates, amphibians, and insects.

BEHAVIOR: This species often forages and roosts in large groups, including with other species of wading birds. During breeding season, the Snowy Egret engages in spectacular courtship dances: bobbing its head wildly as if imitating a slow woodpecker drilling motion; ruffling its wild, voluminous plumes from the crest of its head to the tips of its wings; flying erratically before diving to the ground and rolling all about; and emitting a nearly ceaseless series of raucous calls. These are very much group affairs, with the females watching attentively and occasionally co-participating.

MIGRATE? Yes.

NESTING: Colonial nesters, in trees near wetland habitat. Platform composed of sticks and vegetative debris. About 1 ft. across, or larger.

EGGS: White to pale green-blue. Length of 1 ½ in. Total of 2-5.

FEEDER BEHAVIOR: Does not visit feeders.

COMPARE TO SIMILAR SPECIES: This species is almost like a miniaturized Great Egret, with notable differences including the Snowy's dark bill and yellow feet. In addition, first-year Little Blue Herons may seem similar, but are slimmer, and lack a fully dark bill, yellow feet, and golden yellow coloration between bill and eyes.

DID YOU KNOW? In the late 1800s and (especially) the early 1900s, numerous egret species—including the Snowy—were hunted for their plumes, typically affixed to hats or headdresses for ceremonial court or women's fashion. The term *aigrette* was coined to describe these ornaments, and many were complemented by a variety of gems and adornments of fine tailoring. However, this practice led to a mass reduction in worldwide egret populations, and conservation practices were set in place to restore numbers closer to their previous levels.

J F M A M J J A S O N D

Adults at top and bottom.

Adult in breeding plumage at top (Photo by Dick Daniels / CC BY-SA)
(Note: Nonbreeding plumage features dirty gray streaking along the head and neck),
Subadult at bottom.

⑤ HERRING GULL. *Larus argentatus.*

SIZE: 24 in.

HABITAT: Coastlines, wetlands, landfills, picnic areas.

WILD DIET: Aquatic invertebrates, fish, worms, carrion, garbage at landfills.

BEHAVIOR: Opportunistic, undiscerning forager at the surface of water, in mudflats and tidal areas, at garbage dumps, and sometimes near urban habitation. Often seen milling around large parking lots, piers, and plowed fields, particularly in mixed flocks of gulls. This gull, like the Ring-billed Gull in particular, has adapted remarkably well to human development. Some individuals have been noted to observe humans for extended periods, with possible benefits including the learning and memorization of various urban threats, as well as the mimicking of human food preferences.

MIGRATE? Partially.

NESTING: A cluster of small craters is scraped away in the dirt or sand, one for each individual egg, and lined with vegetation, garbage, and/or feathers. Often hidden behind an obstruction, such as a bush or large rock.

EGGS: Light green-blue to brown with dark speckles. Length of 3 in. Total of 2-3.

FEEDER BEHAVIOR: Does not visit feeders.

COMPARE TO SIMILAR SPECIES: Most similar to Ring-billed Gull. Note the Herring's pale, pink legs, contrasting with the bright yellow legs of the Ring-billed. Also, the Herring is more stockily built, larger, and adults possess a large, red dot on the lower bill.

DID YOU KNOW? As is the case with most gulls, as well as many other seabirds, the Herring Gull can drink salty seawater without complaint. It possesses specialized salt glands near its eyes, which drain directly through the nostrils and allow for the filtered excess salt to be safely secreted. Remarkably, a single gull has the ability to safely filter up to one-quarter of a pound of saline seawater every two hours.

J F M A M J J A S O N D

② **BRANT.** *Branta bernicla.*

SIZE: 24 in.

HABITAT: Oceanic coastlines, marshes, ponds, and sometimes fields.

WILD DIET: Vegetation, both aquatic and terrestrial.

BEHAVIOR: Forages by repeatedly stooping down to pick at grasses and various sources of ground-based vegetation. If on water, the bird will periodically upend itself—always head-first—to reach aquatic grasses and reeds beneath the surface. Normally present in flocks, with benefits to cooperative foraging including increased feeding efficiency, as well as better threat detection. Though ordinarily a coastal goose, this species has been increasingly moving into the interior of the Mid-Atlantic region, primarily due to declines suffered by eelgrass and sea lettuce beds across the neritic, or coastal, North Atlantic.

MIGRATE? Yes.

NESTING: Selects a location on the ground near its feeding grounds. A shallow depression is scratched away, and lined with soft grasses and feathers. About 1 - 1 ½ ft. across.

EGGS: Off-white to pale blue-green. Length of 3 in. Total of 3-5.

FEEDER BEHAVIOR: Does not visit feeders.

COMPARE TO SIMILAR SPECIES: Much smaller than the Canada Goose, with which it occasionally associates. Notice the mostly black neck and head, apart from a thin white band on the neck in adults, and squat stature.

DID YOU KNOW? As the Brant has begun to irregularly forage in habitats farther inland, it appears to follow Canada and Cackling Geese, mimicking some of their feeding and roosting behaviors. Whenever observing a flock of Canada Geese, it is worthwhile to run a quick inspection for any other species (*See* Compare section).

J F M A M J J A S O N D

Adult at top,
Juvenile with Canada Goose at bottom.

Male at top,
Female at bottom (Photo by Jamain / CC BY-SA).

④ **MALLARD.** *Anas platyrhynchos.*

SIZE: 23 in.

HABITAT: Wetlands, shallows of lakes and ponds, parks, and fields.

WILD DIET: Seeds, grains, and human-offered food (though offering food is not recommended). Also, aquatic and terrestrial insects, invertebrates.

BEHAVIOR: This species is a dabbling duck, feeding by dipping its head and neck underwater. Like other waterfowl, this species does not possess teeth inside its bill; instead, it periodically swallows pebbles and gravel, which accumulate in the gizzard and help to churn plant matter into more digestible tidbits. Mallards are adaptable foragers, and will often visit fields or parks where human activity has left food scraps, particularly bread crumbs—though these are not healthy for the birds. In parks with a high degree of human contact, these birds will often be quite comfortable around people.

MIGRATE? Partially.

NESTING: Ground nester. Scrapes a small depression in the ground, upon which loose vegetation and eggs are laid. About 9 in. wide and 3 in. deep.

EGGS: White to light blue-green. Length of 2-2 ½ in. Total of 6-13.

FEEDER BEHAVIOR: Does not visit feeders.

COMPARE TO SIMILAR SPECIES: Male is distinctive, but female can be confused with females of other dabbling duck species. American Black Duck females are darker in the body than female Mallards, and also have a dull green tint to the bill.

DID YOU KNOW? Mallards are known for readily breeding with ducks of other species, producing hybrid offspring that can prove an unusual challenge to identify. Species that have hybridized with Mallards include Northern Shovelers (e.g., producing Northern Shoveler x Mallard offspring), Wood Ducks, Northern Pintails, Common Eiders, Green-winged Teals, Gadwalls, and many others.

J F M A M J J A S O N D

63

② OSPREY. *Pandion haliaetus.*

SIZE: 23 in.

HABITAT: Lakes, bays, rivers, and wetlands.

WILD DIET: Fish (less than 18 in. in length).

BEHAVIOR: When hunting, flies as high as 100 feet above areas of shallow water (with wings held in an M-shape), searching for prey below. Once spotted, the individual enters a steep, aerodynamic dive with talons outstretched, piercing the surface of the water upon impact and grasping the fish. This process is repeated with remarkable efficiency; when an osprey is situated in a habitat with sufficient food sources, it frequently seizes a fish in just 10 minutes, and a few dives, of hunting. Often also called seahawks, bayhawks, riverhawks, and fish-hawks, referencing their distinct ecological niche.

MIGRATE? Yes.

NESTING: Selects a high fork of a tree, a clifftop, or a manmade nesting platform. A loose, roughshod platform of sticks. May be reused. About 3-5 ft. wide and up to 3 ft. deep after many years of use and additions.

EGGS: Light yellow-brown with red or brown splotches. Length of 2 ½ in. Total of 1-4.

FEEDER BEHAVIOR: Does not visit feeders.

COMPARE TO SIMILAR SPECIES: Much smaller than the Bald Eagle. If observed in an area with many gulls present, notice the distinct markings of this species; additionally, if carrying prey, the Osprey holds fish in its talons—rather than gulls, which hold prey with their bills.

DID YOU KNOW? Ospreys are one of the only raptor species in the world with a reversible outer toe, which allows for this species to have two toes on both the front and back when gripping slimy, wet fish prey. They also possess small, barb-like grips on the pads of their feet, which allow for an even more secure hold.

J F M A M J J A S O N D

Adults with fresh kill at top and bottom.

Adult at top (Photo by Charles J. Sharp / CC BY-SA / Cropped),
Juvenile at bottom.

① **GLOSSY IBIS.** *Plegadis falcinellus.*

SIZE: 23 in.

HABITAT: Shallow wetlands, ponds, and streams; fields.

WILD DIET: Aquatic invertebrates, insects and spiders, reptiles, amphibians, fish, and occasionally grains.

BEHAVIOR: Like the White Ibis, this species frequently flocks when foraging, roosting, and anytime in between. Individuals carefully probe throughout the bottom of the water column, stirring up organic matter and quickly nabbing any potential prey items. This activity may bring flocking waders, such as Snowy Egrets, to investigate. Flocks will often fly in V-formation between feeding and roosting sites, the latter of which can draw hundreds of birds to perch in the subcanopies of wetland swamps and mangrove stands.

MIGRATE? Yes.

NESTING: Colonial nester, nesting in trees at a low to medium height. A messy stick platform is arranged for the year's brood. About 1 ft. wide.

EGGS: Pale to bright blue-green. Length of 2 in. Total of 2-5.

FEEDER BEHAVIOR: Does not visit feeders.

COMPARE TO SIMILAR SPECIES: Adult's dark coloration and trademark sickle-shaped bill distinguish from most other wading birds. White-faced Ibis has red coloration between the bill and eye, rather than the dark coloration observable in the Glossy—both of which are clearly outlined in white.

DID YOU KNOW? Glossy Ibises tend to wander more than other species from their established natural range, particularly if current locations are not providing sufficient amounts of food. This has led to a colonization pattern over the past century that has stretched up much of the Atlantic coast, regularly treating Northern birders to the bright colors often reserved for neotropical avifauna.

J F M A M J J A S O N D

② RED-BREASTED MERGANSER.
Mergus serrator.

SIZE: 22 in.

HABITAT: Coastlines of oceans, large lakes (e.g., Great Lakes), and large rivers.

WILD DIET: Mostly small fish, but also aquatic invertebrates and amphibians.

BEHAVIOR: A diving duck, this species dives with a soft, deft jump from its floating position into the depths below. It usually hunts minnow-sized fish, consuming up to two dozen each day. Group hunting tactics are sometimes used, wherein a group of schooling fish is herded into shallower waters by an arc-shaped formation of mergansers.

MIGRATE? Yes.

NESTING: Nests on the ground in a well-sheltered location, sometimes near a fallen tree. A shallow depression is formed, upon which loose vegetation and feathers are placed. About 1 ft. across.

EGGS: Off-white. Length of 2 ½ in. Total of 4-16.

FEEDER BEHAVIOR: Does not visit feeders.

COMPARE TO SIMILAR SPECIES: Common Merganser also has males with green heads and females with red heads, with a similar silhouette. However, male Common Mergansers have a white body (apart from upper back) and lack a reddish breast; meanwhile, male Red-breasteds have brown and white sides, a trailing tuft on the head, and a white stripe on the neck *with a red-brown upper chest*. In addition, female Red-breasteds have paler head and neck coloration than their Common counterparts.

DID YOU KNOW? Among the merganser species, the Red-breasted has the greatest affinity for larger bodies of water, including oceans and the Great Lakes.

J F M A M J J A S O N D

Male at top,
Female at bottom.

Male at top (Photo by Dick Daniels / CC BY-SA),
Female at bottom (Photo by Dick Daniels / CC BY-SA).

② **AMERICAN BLACK DUCK.** *Anas rubripes.*

SIZE: 22 in.
HABITAT: Wetlands.
WILD DIET: Aquatic vegetation and invertebrates.
BEHAVIOR: A dabbling duck, this species will repeatedly upend itself when foraging. This species is somewhat unique, however, in that it will sometimes dive as well—both to avoid predators and to reach vegetation in deeper waters. Individuals often have a strong affinity to their usual wintering sites, occasionally starving rather than leaving a frozen-over wetland that has been visited in past years. Additionally, like other dabbling ducks, the American Black Duck can take flight directly from a floating position, allowing for a quick getaway from any perceived threat; this is unlike the behavior of diving ducks, which frequently must perform a running start while sufficient momentum is generated for flight.
MIGRATE? Partially.
NESTING: Nests on the ground in a well-sheltered location, or very occasionally in tree cavities. A shallow depression is formed, upon which loose vegetation and feathers are placed.
EGGS: White. Length of 2 ½ in. Total of 8-14, occasionally with a second brood.
FEEDER BEHAVIOR: Does not visit feeders.

COMPARE TO SIMILAR SPECIES: Darker than Mallards, with a duller bill color. Darker than Mottled Duck, with a brown head (rather than tan). Gadwall is smaller with a gray body in males, and a moderately brown body in females.

DID YOU KNOW? Though not yet on the roster of endangered species, this duck has experienced declines as steep as 90% over the past half-century. This may largely owe to the fact that its preferred wooded wetland habitats are increasingly scarce due to deforestation and human development.

J F M A M J J A S O N D

③ **RED-TAILED HAWK.** *Buteo jamaicensis.*

SIZE: 22 in.

HABITAT: Nearly anywhere, but prefers open woods, fields, and roadsides.

WILD DIET: Mostly small mammals (in particular, squirrels). Less frequently, birds, reptiles, and carrion.

BEHAVIOR: Often observed soaring or circling gracefully in the sky, with light wingbeats, though individuals also perch in trees or on telephone poles. While driving along a highway or interstate, this species is commonly present in perches along the roadside—much more visible in winter, after most leaves have fallen. The Red-tailed Hawk, like many raptors, possesses phenomenal visual acuity; a lone squirrel darting through brush and long grass can be spotted from up to 300 feet away. Once its quarry has been sighted, the hawk swoops low with strong wingbeats, culminating with a forceful strike of the talons, which may stun the prey. Upon its secure capture, the hawk normally carries its prey to a safe perch for consumption. Its familiar, piercing call is often heard in the background of Western-genre films, and is usually given in flight.

MIGRATE? Partially.

NESTING: Typically situated atop a large tree or similarly habitable human-made structure (e.g., billboards). Piles of sticks up to 3 ft. across, and up to 5 ft. deep.

EGGS: White, with some brown blotching. Length of 2 ½ in. Total of 2-5.

FEEDER BEHAVIOR: Uncommonly hunts near feeders.

COMPARE TO SIMILAR SPECIES: Similar to Red-shouldered Hawk in shape, but note pale undersides, dark band of streaking across upper belly, and light red coloration on underside of tail.

DID YOU KNOW? The ancient practice of falconry, whereby humans train captive raptors to hunt animals on their behalf, is continued today by nearly 5,000 Americans—who must first secure a regulatory permit and a registered sponsor. The Red-tailed Hawk, along with the Red-shouldered Hawk, is one of only two North American hawks approved for use by trainees or apprentices; consequently, the Red-tailed is also the most common raptor used by North American falconers, with some hawks adapting to trained hunting techniques in a mere two weeks.

J F M A M J J A S O N D

Perching adult at top,
Soaring adult at bottom (Photo by Tom Koerner / CC BY-SA).

Perching adult at top (Photo by James E. Smallwood / CC BY-SA),
Soaring juvenile at bottom (Photo by Bettina Arrigoni / CC BY-SA / Cropped).

① **RED-SHOULDERED HAWK.** *Buteo lineatus.*

SIZE: 21 in.

HABITAT: Open woods, flooded woods.

WILD DIET: Mostly small mammals (such as mice and chipmunks), as well as birds, reptiles, and fish.

BEHAVIOR: The Red-shouldered Hawk tends to hunt more frequently from a perch than its Red-tailed counterpart, but individuals may also be occasionally observed circling and soaring in the open skies. When hunting, the Red-shouldered often finds a semi-concealed perch in a grove of trees, monitoring the gaps in the forest floor for any ground-dwellers brave enough to reveal themselves. After a low, powerful swoop and a downward strike of the talons, the hawk secures its catch and consumes from a nearby perch.

MIGRATE? Partially.

NESTING: Typically situated in the fork of a deciduous tree, near but not at the top. Piles of sticks up to 2 ft. across and 3 ft. deep, depending on the geometry of the fork.

EGGS: White with some brown blotching. Length of 2 in. Total of 3-5.

FEEDER BEHAVIOR: Uncommonly hunts near feeders.

COMPARE TO SIMILAR SPECIES: Similar to Red-tailed Hawk in shape, but note the red present on the upper chest (present in adults) and the black-and-white striped pattern on the underside of its tail (present in both adults and juveniles).

DID YOU KNOW? As recently as the early 1900s, this species was among the most common of all North American raptors. However, the deforestation and clearing of mature woodland across the U.S. has led to a significant drop in Red-shouldered Hawk numbers, which has correlated with a rise in Red-tailed Hawk numbers. This shift is directly attributable to the habitats preferred by each species, with Red-tailed typically found in more open country and Red-shouldereds in wooded areas.

J F M A M J J A S O N D

75

② GADWALL. *Mareca strepera.*

SIZE: 20 in.

HABITAT: Wetlands.

WILD DIET: Mostly aquatic vegetation, also aquatic invertebrates and insects.

BEHAVIOR: A dabbling duck, this species periodically upends itself while foraging—stretching its head and neck below the water surface to wrest vegetative matter from the shallows. Individuals may combatively approach other species of waterfowl to steal their catch, and linger near the fringes of flocks to facilitate this behavior. Aside from these interactions, however, Gadwalls tend to form smaller flocks than other, more sociable duck species. On another note, while most birds determine the arrangement of yearly mating pairs in the springtime, this species actually performs all of its courtship displays in late fall. Drake and hen are thereafter closely coupled, and may even shyly romance each other with an eye to the following year's breeding period.

MIGRATE? Partially.

NESTING: Nests within sight of water, at a site obscured by thick underbrush. Scrapes a small impression in the dirt, and fills with small twigs. About 1 - 1 ½ ft. across.

EGGS: White to off-white. Length of 2 in. Total of 8-13.

FEEDER BEHAVIOR: Does not visit feeders.

COMPARE TO SIMILAR SPECIES: Male has a grayish body and drab head, which are distinctive upon inspection. Females are similar to Mallards and related species, but lack any colored wing patch (theirs is white instead), and have a more squarely shaped head.

DID YOU KNOW? Gadwalls are widely distributed globally, with well-established populations in North America from Alaska to Mexico, and in Eurasia from Iceland to Japan. There have also been irregular sightings of this species throughout the Caribbean, in northern Oceania, and in North Africa. In total, the total worldwide population stands at nearly 5 million individuals.

J F M A M J J A S O N D

Male at top left and female at top right,
Adults dabbling at bottom.

Breeding male at top,
Female with ducklings at bottom.

② **WOOD DUCK.** *Aix sponsa.*

SIZE: 20 in.

HABITAT: Wetlands and small waterways.

WILD DIET: Nuts, seeds, and berries; also, some aquatic invertebrates and insects.

BEHAVIOR: Forages by dabbling in the shallows or by slowly, adroitly walking on land. Tends to prefer sheltered habitats that offer plenty of shelter from predators, such as large raptors. Like other dabbling ducks which ply their trade in secluded wetlands, this species is flushed easily by human activity.

MIGRATE? Mostly.

NESTING: Cavity nester. Natural hollows of mature trees (near water) are usually selected, often dozens of feet off the ground. The entry hole may be as small as 4-6 in. in diameter, but this species can adapt to a variety of cavity sizes. Lined with ample feathers.

EGGS: White to off-white. Length of 2 in. Total of 7-17, with 1-2 broods.

FEEDER BEHAVIOR: Does not visit feeders, but uses nest boxes.

COMPARE TO SIMILAR SPECIES: Male is very distinctive in breeding plumage. Nonbreeding and eclipse (molting, occurs during summer) males have washed-out coloration, and usually no green on head. Meanwhile, females have a noticeable white eye patch which extends toward the back of the head.

DID YOU KNOW? As with other duck species, male Wood Ducks are known as drakes, and females as hens. All ducks undergo full molts of their flight feathers during the warmer months, which render them completely flightless for several weeks. In order to better avoid predation and other perceived threats, dabbling ducks such as the Wood Duck tend to situate themselves in the densely vegetated corners of marshes for this period, which provide ample cover. Accordingly, the more brightly colored drakes display a washed-out eclipse plumage during this time to provide better concealment.

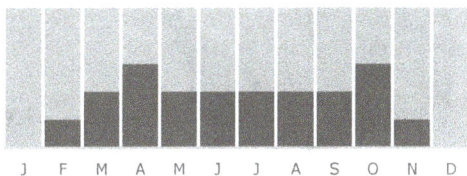

J F M A M J J A S O N D

① **AMERICAN WIGEON.** *Mareca americana.*

SIZE: 20 in.

HABITAT: Wetlands, lakes, and ponds. Also, suburban fields and lawns.

WILD DIET: Mostly vegetation, both aquatic and terrestrial.

BEHAVIOR: A dabbling duck, this species forages by upending itself in the water, with its tail pointed nearly straight up to the sky. Its diet—which is among the most strictly vegetarian of all dabbling ducks—also consists of grasses grazed from fields, lawns, and grasslands. The American Wigeon's stubby, almost goose-like bill is uniquely adapted to this form of terrestrial grazing, though it also provides ample leverage when harvesting submerged, underwater grasses. Flocks begin to migrate south as the leaves turn color, as they require a stable source of green foodstuffs year round. Individuals may also loosely associate with foraging flocks of American Coots.

MIGRATE? Yes.

NESTING: Selects a location in grasslands, somewhat near water. A small impression is excavated, after which the nest is lined with twigs and grasses. About 6-9 in. across.

EGGS: Milky white. Length of 2 in. Total of 5-12.

FEEDER BEHAVIOR: Does not visit feeders.

COMPARE TO SIMILAR SPECIES: Male has a distinctive green patch of coloration from its eye to the back of its head, and also features a white head crown. Females have the stubby bill of the male, in addition to a dark patch around the eye.

DID YOU KNOW? This species is a close cousin of the Eurasian Wigeon, which—though native to Europe, Asia, and North Africa—has been known to appear as a somewhat uncommon vagrant throughout the United States and southern Canada. Eurasian males have a chestnut colored head with a whitish-tan patch on the crest, while females often have a more reddish-brown head.

J F M A M J J A S O N D

Male at top,
Female and male at bottom.

Wintering male at top (Photo by Sammy Sam / CC BY-SA / Cropped),
Wintering female at bottom (Photo by Russ / CC BY-SA / Cropped).

① **LONG-TAILED DUCK.** *Clangula hyemalis.*

SIZE: 20 in.

HABITAT: Coastlines of oceans and the Great Lakes. Sometimes offshore.

WILD DIET: Mostly aquatic invertebrates.

BEHAVIOR: Aside from nesting, this species spends nearly all of its time on the water, whether roosting or foraging. Individuals dive over 200 feet beneath the water's surface in search of prey—though usually, closer to depths of 25 or 30 feet—and submerge for long intervals repeatedly throughout the day. Unlike most other ducks, but similar to some other aquatic birds such as penguins, Long-tailed Ducks swim underwater by flapping their wings, rather than by paddling with their webbed feet. Flocks may remain offshore for extended periods of time, roosting and feeding in the open ocean; however, many individuals seem to prefer more sheltered bays, especially during stormy weather.

MIGRATE? Yes.

NESTING: Colonial nesters, usually very localized on shorelines in the Arctic or upper subarctic. A shallow depression is excavated, upon which leaves, grasses, and feathers are laid. About 15 in. across.

EGGS: White to off-white. Length of 2 in. Total of 6-7.

FEEDER BEHAVIOR: Does not visit feeders.

COMPARE TO SIMILAR SPECIES: Very distinctive markings, but male's long tail may vaguely resemble that of the male Northern Pintail (which is almost always found in much shallower, often wetland habitats).

DID YOU KNOW? The Long-tailed Duck is classified as vulnerable to endangered by many species conservation organizations, but the associated reasons are as yet unclear. Possible explanations include the following: ecological changes due to global warming, the growing presence of lead in the food chain, fishing net entanglements, melting sea ice floes (the edges of which are frequently used as staging points for dives), and the effects of invasive species of aquatic invertebrates (particularly in the Great Lakes).

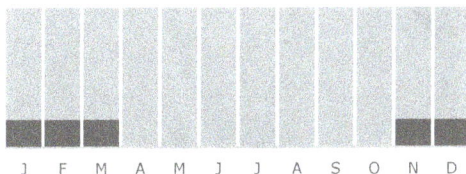

J F M A M J J A S O N D

83

① **SURF SCOTER.** *Melanitta perspicillata.*

SIZE: 19 in.

HABITAT: Winters on coastlines of oceans and the Great Lakes, and mostly stops at larger lakes and reservoirs during migration.

WILD DIET: Mostly aquatic invertebrates, particularly from the seafloor.

BEHAVIOR: Congregates in very large flocks during migration and wintering, and is normally observed within 500 feet of shore, at depths of less than 25 to 30 feet. This species dives rather than dabbles, and forages at the bottom of the water column for invertebrates, such as mussels and snails. Dives are taken with powerful strokes of the paddled feet, while the wings are held partially open to provide directional stability.

MIGRATE? Yes.

NESTING: Selects a site hidden amid dense vegetation, near a seacoast, lake, or wetland. A bowl is scraped into the ground and lined with feathers and loose vegetation. About 1 ft. across.

EGGS: White. Length of 2 ½ in. Total of 6-8.

FEEDER BEHAVIOR: Does not visit feeders.

COMPARE TO SIMILAR SPECIES: Resembles other species of scoters, but males have large white patches on the top and back of the head, and females have a dark head cap and patchy cheeks. Black Scoter males have no white patches on the head, and females have a dark head cap *with fully pale neck and cheeks*. Male White-winged Scoters have a white eye patch and females lack a dark crest on top of head; also, both sexes of White-winged usually have a visible white wing patch.

DID YOU KNOW? While the Surf Scoter may occasionally eat some forms of aquatic vegetation, it is able to efficiently siphon out its invertebrate prey without consuming any plant growth. This trait is necessary to maximize nutritional intake on each dive.

Male at top,
Female at bottom.

Male at top (Photo by Don Faulkner / CC BY-SA / Cropped),
Female at bottom (Photo by Matt Osborne / CC BY-SA).

① **BLACK SCOTER.** *Melanitta americana.*

SIZE: 19 in.

HABITAT: Winters on coastlines of oceans and the Great Lakes, and mostly stops at larger lakes and reservoirs during migration.

WILD DIET: Aquatic invertebrates, insects, fish eggs, and sometimes aquatic vegetation.

BEHAVIOR: Not quite as numerous as the related Surf Scoter, the Black Scoter may occur in same-species or interspecies flocks. Individuals repeatedly dive below the surface to forage, often preferring depths of less than 40 feet; this affords the duck a longer period during which to wrest its prey from the seafloor, with prey items often including well-anchored bivalves (e.g., mussels). When diving, individuals tend to paddle with their feet, and do not partially open their wings like other scoters: although reasons for this difference remain unclear.

MIGRATE? Yes.

NESTING: Selects a grassy site close to shore. A bowl is scraped into the ground and lined with feathers. About 1 ft. across.

EGGS: White. Length of 2 ½ in. Total of 6-8.

FEEDER BEHAVIOR: Does not visit feeders.

COMPARE TO SIMILAR SPECIES: For males, their all-black coloration and bright orange knob at the base of bill are distinctive among sea ducks and scoters. The female possesses a dark head cap, as well as pale neck and cheeks. These help to distinguish from other similar species, such as the Surf Scoter.

DID YOU KNOW? The Black Scoter is native to North America and northeastern Russia; its close relative, the Common Scoter, is native to much of northern and western Eurasia. However, they have only recently been classified as separate species: the conclusive differences include bill coloration (the male Common has a duller colored bill) and mating calls.

J F M A M J J A S O N D

⑤ **RING-BILLED GULL.** *Larus delawarensis.*

SIZE: 19 in.

HABITAT: Coastlines, wetlands, landfills, picnic areas.

WILD DIET: Insects, fish, worms, grains, rodents, garbage at landfills.

BEHAVIOR: Forages at the surface of water, in mudflats and tidal areas, at garbage dumps, and sometimes near urban habitation. Often seen milling about or orderly standing in large parking lots and on piers. Individuals tend to exhibit an uncanny degree of resourcefulness, with a highly varied diet and a well-adapted lifestyle to the modern Anthropocene. Individuals may regularly visit the dumpsters near picnic areas or fast-food restaurants, seeking out food scraps and even the small flying insects which gather overhead. In areas with higher degrees of human contact, Ring-billed Gulls have been known to approach humans for food, even nabbing unguarded morsels from outdoor benches and tables.

MIGRATE? Partially.

NESTING: Nests in groups of up to many thousands on sand, concrete, and rocky beaches. Little to no nest lining.

EGGS: Light blue-green to light brown, with dark splotching. Length of 2 ½ in. Total of 3.

FEEDER BEHAVIOR: Does not visit feeders.

COMPARE TO SIMILAR SPECIES: Most similar to Herring Gull. Note the Ring-billed's bright, yellow legs, contrasted with the pale, pink legs of the Herring Gull. Ring-billed Gulls are also smaller, more slight of build, and are most likely to have a sharply defined black ring near the end of the bill.

DID YOU KNOW? Ring-billed Gulls are able to accurately sense their magnetic bearings as soon as they are a few days old. This navigational aptitude allows them to accurately judge the correct direction for their migration routes.

J F M A M J J A S O N D

Adult in breeding plumage at top (Photo by Mdf / CC BY-SA / Cropped),
Adult in nonbreeding plumage at bottom (Notice light, dirty streaking on head and neck).

Breeding male at top,
Nonbreeding males at center,
Female at bottom.

① **NORTHERN SHOVELER.** *Spatula clypeata.*

SIZE: 19 in.

HABITAT: Mostly wetlands, also lakes and ponds during fall and winter.

WILD DIET: Aquatic invertebrates and algae. Uncommonly, aquatic vegetation.

BEHAVIOR: A dabbling duck, this species forages by upending itself in the shallows as it forages for prey. More commonly, individuals also swim with their bills skimming, sweeping, or partially submerged beneath the water surface. The notched edges of its inner bill act like a sieve, allowing for invertebrates—including organisms as small as plankton—to be efficiently filtered from the water. Consequently, this duck is adaptable to varying qualities of wetland habitat, allowing individuals to forage in wetland areas which might not have sufficient nutrients for other dabbling ducks. Shovelers may flock in small groups, but are less likely to do so than many other dabbling ducks. Occasionally, this species may be observed walking or roosting on land.

MIGRATE? Yes.

NESTING: Selects a grassy site near wetlands. A bowl is scraped into the ground and lined with twigs, vegetation, and feathers. Up to 1 ft. across.

EGGS: White to off-white. Length of 2 in. Total of 8-11.

FEEDER BEHAVIOR: Does not visit feeders.

COMPARE TO SIMILAR SPECIES: Best distinguished by the long, wide, and shovel-like bill present in all individuals of this species, though the female's drab coloration may initially resemble that of other waterfowl.

DID YOU KNOW? When incubating females of this species are threatened by nest predators, they quickly defecate on the eggs before fleeing. This may serve one of two purposes: concealing the appearance and smell of the eggs, or deterring the predator from consuming a potentially disease-ridden meal.

J F M A M J J A S O N D

① **ROYAL TERN.** *Thalasseus maximus.*

SIZE: 19 in.

HABITAT: Oceanic coastlines, particularly sheltered bays and estuaries.

WILD DIET: Mostly small fish (e.g., anchovies), also small crabs and shrimp.

BEHAVIOR: Frequently flies near shore when foraging, preferring calmer stretches of water. When suitable prey is sighted, the tern will hover with wings outstretched as it prepares to plunge headfirst. Interestingly, this hunting technique is modified when dealing with crabs and flying fish; in these instances, the chasseur must instead swoop low over the water as it makes a stealthier approach.

MIGRATE? Yes.

NESTING: Colonial nester, usually on beaches or islands. A spartan affair, a nest scrape is lined with little to no vegetation. Depth may be less than 1 in.

EGGS: Light brown, blue, or olive with dark mottling and/or smudging. Length of 2 ½ in. Total of 1-2.

FEEDER BEHAVIOR: Does not visit feeders.

COMPARE TO SIMILAR SPECIES: Long, pointed bill characteristic of terns, in addition to bright orange bill coloration and streamlined head profile, quickly distinguish from gulls. Among terns, only the Caspian Tern is of similarly large size. The Royal lacks the Caspian's fully dark underwing feathers at the tips (usually just a dark outline on the edges), and has a white forehead from late summer through winter. It is also of slightly daintier profile.

DID YOU KNOW? Though terns are known to suffer from *kleptoparasitism*, or the stealing of prey after capture by another species, the Royal Tern has itself been observed harrying pelicans—which outweigh the tern by an approximate factor of eight—for an easy catch.

J F M A M J J A S O N D

Nonbreeding adults (Notice bare forehead) at top,
Breeding adult scanning water at bottom (Photo by Melissa McMasters / CC BY-SA / Cropped).

Adult male at top,
Adult female at middle,
Juvenile at bottom.

① **NORTHERN HARRIER.** *Circus hudsonius.*

SIZE: 19 in.
HABITAT: Mostly open country. Breeds in wetlands.
WILD DIET: Small mammals (e.g., voles, mice, and shrews), small birds (e.g., sparrows), reptiles and amphibians, and occasionally large insects.
BEHAVIOR: Solitary glider over the ground with wings held in a V-shape, typically seeking out small rodent prey. Occasional quick, strong flaps allow the harrier to remain aloft as it circles and explores its feeding grounds. When movement is sighted, it will briefly contort its body as it enters a predatory dive. During migration—which, in fall, occurs much later than most other migrating raptors—harriers are a common sight in the skies, soaring with steady wingbeats and often holding their wings in a shallower V-shape than when hunting. During the winter, individuals flock together at nighttime roosts, which may be situated directly on the ground in fields.
MIGRATE? Yes.
NESTING: Nests on the ground in wetlands, usually concealed from view. Platform of reeds and twigs. Nearly 2 ft. across.
EGGS: Off-white to light blue. Length of 2 in. Total of 3-7.
FEEDER BEHAVIOR: Does not visit feeders.

COMPARE TO SIMILAR SPECIES: Owl-like facial features and dihedral (V-shaped) wing shape while gliding are most diagnostic for this species. In addition, each individual displays a prominent white rump, directly above the tail feathers.

DID YOU KNOW? Northern Harriers are polygynous breeders, meaning that each male mates with multiple females over the course of the breeding season. This consequently makes for a busy period of hunting in the late spring as hatchlings from each of the male's sired nests must be duly fed.

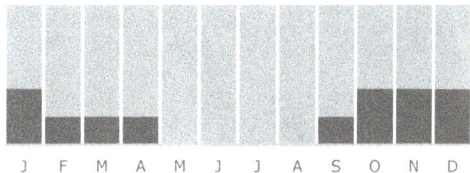

J F M A M J J A S O N D

⑤ AMERICAN CROW. *Corvus brachyrhynchos.*

SIZE: 19 in.

HABITAT: Nearly anywhere, but especially open woods.

WILD DIET: Nearly anything, including nuts and fruits, grains and seeds, eggs and hatchlings, insects and spiders, worms, mice, carrion, and garbage.

BEHAVIOR: Highly intelligent. Engages in sophisticated communication, problem-solving, and self-governing behavior in groups. Often observed in flocks, also known as murders (e.g., a murder of crows).

MIGRATE? No.

NESTING: Hidden in a fork near the trunk of a tree, and near the tree's apex. Cup-shaped, formed from twigs and lined with vegetation. Usually about 1 ft. wide and 6 in. deep.

EGGS: Shades of blue-green, with speckling. Length of 1 ½ in. Total of 3-6.

BIRD FEEDING TIPS

FEEDER DIET: Black-oil and hulled sunflower seeds, suet, oats, cracked corn, peanuts and peanut hearts, millet, milo, fruit. **FEEDER TYPES**: Ground, platforms. **FEEDER BEHAVIOR**: Large size may intimidate some birds upon arrival. Tends to have a large appetite, which proves problematic for some feeder setups, and may take excess food to store elsewhere.

COMPARE TO SIMILAR SPECIES: Most similar to Common Raven, but smaller. Smooth head and throat feathers, while tail is more fan-shaped than wedge-shaped when unfurled. Also, note the characteristic *caw, caw* calls which are familiar across much of the U.S.

DID YOU KNOW? Among many other examples of tool use, crows have taken discarded, still-lit cigarettes and rubbed them inside of their wings to kill parasites; sharpened sticks to poke between fence posts, so as to feed on hidden insects, seeds, and grains; and rewarded humans who set out food with shiny trinkets that they carried from nearby.

J F M A M J J A S O N D

Perching adult at top (Photo by Becky Matsubara / CC BY-SA / Cropped),
Flying adult at bottom.

Adults at top and bottom.

② **AMERICAN OYSTERCATCHER.**
Haematopus palliatus.

SIZE: 18 in.

HABITAT: Oceanic coastlines, including nearby islands. Specifically, muddy tidal flats, beaches, and saltmarshes.

WILD DIET: Oysters, mussels, clams. Occasionally, starfish, crabs, sea urchins, and worms.

BEHAVIOR: Walks or darts deliberately in the shallows or on beaches, with frequent investigative pauses as it seeks out its prey. When dealing with bivalves (i.e., two-shelled mollusks, such as clams), it must swiftly insert its bill in the opening between the prey's shells and sever its adductor muscles; if this is not accomplished sufficiently quickly, the mollusk exacts its revenge by tightly grasping the oystercatcher's bill and anchoring it in place, amid the omnipresent dangers of changing tides. Outside of hunting hours, individuals are frequently observed preening their feathers.

MIGRATE? Yes.

NESTING: Located on beaches or near saltmarshes. An impression is formed in the sand roughly the size of the bird's underside. About 8 in. across.

EGGS: Off-white with brown speckling. Length of 2 - 2 ½ in. Total of 2-3.

FEEDER BEHAVIOR: Does not visit feeders.

COMPARE TO SIMILAR SPECIES: Highly distinctive among oceanic shorebirds, particularly owing to its bright red bill.

DID YOU KNOW? Individual oystercatchers often perfect their own brand of confronting prey. Some use their bills as levers to open shells, and others attempt to break apart the protective shell—with varying degrees of caution appearing to be used with each method.

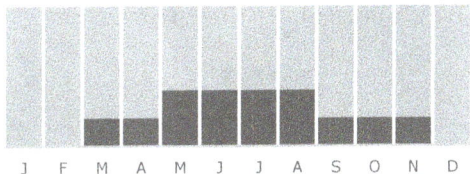

J F M A M J J A S O N D

① **PEREGRINE FALCON.** *Falco peregrinus.*

SIZE: 18 in.

HABITAT: Coastlines, mountains and valleys, and cities.

WILD DIET: Mostly medium-sized birds (e.g., pigeons, ducks, and gulls); also bats.

BEHAVIOR: Often watching for prey from an elevated perch or from high in the sky. Once prey is sighted, this bird enters a steep dive, reaching speeds of over 240 mph, culminating in a quick strike-and-kill. May also pursue prey from lower heights, flying up to 70 mph horizontally in pursuit: though cruising speeds are often just 30 to 40 mph. Individuals may periodically specialize in certain modes of hunting, depending on dietary needs and habitat characteristics. Some have been known to regularly soar high and dive upon Blue Jays, producing a puff of airborne feathers upon impact, while others have perched near inlets of bays, eagerly awaiting flocks of coots or ducks to unsuspectingly approach. Peregrines are increasingly taking up residence in urban environments, where they hunt pigeons and regularly nest on skyscraper ledges, the latter simulating its natural preference for cliffside nesting.

MIGRATE? Partially.

NESTING: Cliffside ledges. The topsoil is scraped away to form a shallow indentation. About 8 in. across.

EGGS: Off-white to red-brown, with splotchiness. Length of 2 in. Total of 2-4.

FEEDER BEHAVIOR: Does not visit feeders.

COMPARE TO SIMILAR SPECIES: Pointed, swept-back wings differentiate from other birds of prey, such as hawks or eagles. Among falconids, much larger than the Merlin and American Kestrel.

DID YOU KNOW? Like a guided missile, the Peregrine Falcon is able to make minute, controlled adjustments to the direction and camber of its dive to more accurately strike its moving targets. Aeronautical engineers have studied these characteristics for decades in order to understand the potential applications for aircraft, drones, and missiles. This is an example of *biomimicry*, wherein human engineering is modelled after materials or behaviors observed in the animal kingdom—which makes plenty of sense, considering the degree of specialization that each animal must possess to best exploit its well-honed ecological niche.

J F M A M J J A S O N D

Perching adult at top (Photo by Mosharaf Hossain / CC BY-SA / Cropped),
Flying adult at bottom (Photo by Andy Reago, Chrissy McClarren / CC BY-SA / Cropped).

Adult at top (Photo by Andreas Trepte / CC BY-SA / Cropped)
Adults skimming at bottom.

① **BLACK SKIMMER.** *Rynchops niger.*

SIZE: 18 in.

HABITAT: Oceanic coastlines and bays. Occasionally present in nearby wetlands.

WILD DIET: Small fish (e.g., anchovies, herring), shrimp, and crabs.

BEHAVIOR: Skimmers feed by flying slightly above the water surface with long bill open and head extended; the mandible, or lower section of bill, is held below the surface in search of small prey. This tactile approach to hunting is highly unique, and the Black Skimmer is able to snap its jaws shut in a fraction of second once any potential prey makes contact with the lower bill. This species' hunting technique requires relatively calm waters to avoid buffeting by heavy waves, and individuals have been observed feeding at all times of day and night, but particularly at sunrise and sunset. Low wing-loading allows for graceful flight.

MIGRATE? Yes.

NESTING: Loose colonial nester. Selects a beachside location on a protected section of coastline or island. May cohabitate with various species of tern. A shallow impression is scraped into the sand or soil, upon which eggs are laid. About 8 in. across.

EGGS: Off-white, with dark splotches. Length of 2 in. Total of 2-5.

FEEDER BEHAVIOR: Does not visit feeders.

COMPARE TO SIMILAR SPECIES: Highly distinctive among other seabirds, particularly once bill is observed.

DID YOU KNOW? The tendency of Black Skimmers to hunt in twilight, also known as *crepuscularity*, is shared by some other avian species, such as the Chimney Swift and American Woodcock. This may confer this species an advantage when sharing particularly active hunting grounds with other birds which instead hunt primarily by light.

J F M A M J J A S O N D

103

② HOODED MERGANSER. *Lophodytes cucullatus.*

SIZE: 18 in.

HABITAT: Wetlands, ponds, small lakes and rivers. Occasionally, coastal bays.

WILD DIET: Mostly fish and aquatic invertebrates. Also, small amphibians, insects, and aquatic vegetation.

BEHAVIOR: This species typically congregates in small groups on protected bodies of water, irregularly diving beneath the surface to forage for prey. When diving, the merganser half-leaps from its floating position into the water, producing a clean entrance with minimal surface disturbance—which is important for maintaining its cover when hunting. This duck is able to change directions quickly while underwater, and even observe its surroundings in the most turbid of conditions. Like other mergansers, this species has minute serrations on the lining of its bill, which assist with grasping and securing underwater prey.

MIGRATE? Yes.

NESTING: Cavity nester, using natural or woodpecker-manufactured hollows in trees, as well as nest boxes. Lined with feathers. Entrance less than 6 in. wide.

EGGS: White to off-white, and somewhat spherical. Length of 2 in. Total of 7-13.

FEEDER BEHAVIOR: Does not visit feeders, but uses nest boxes.

COMPARE TO SIMILAR SPECIES: Males have a white head marking resembling that of the Bufflehead, but the rest of its markings are very different. Females may vaguely resemble other merganser species, but Hoodeds are much smaller and possess a more noticeable tuft at the rear of the head.

DID YOU KNOW? Hooded Mergansers have been observed repeatedly throughout the past decade in Dublin, Ireland, but it is likely that these are captive escapees and that they have not yet established a viable breeding population.

J F M A M J J A S O N D

Male at top,
Male and female at bottom.

Adults at top and bottom.

① PILEATED WOODPECKER. *Dryocopus pileatus.*

SIZE: 18 in.

HABITAT: Dense, mature woods. Sometimes, semi-open woods and wooded suburbs.

WILD DIET: Mostly insects (in particular, carpenter ants), also some nuts and fruits.

BEHAVIOR: Clings to tree bark while boring into the wood. Individuals may excavate deeply into the trunk, forming ovaline hollows recognizable long after the woodpecker has passed through. These forays are often intended to root out ant colonies; the woodpecker's long, extensible tongue is highly sensitive, and acts both as a tactile antenna and a dexterous tool for rooting out food sources (*See* Photo at bottom left). Occasionally forages at ground level. Likely sparse across its habitat, as individual breeding pairs aggressively defend a territory of several hundred acres from other conspecifics: with loud drilling often used as a signaling mechanism to potential rivals.

MIGRATE? No.

NESTING: Inside dead trees, where a round-entranced cavity is bored 1-2 ft. deep.

EGGS: Milky white with light spotting. Length of 1 ¼ in. Total of 3-5.

BIRD FEEDING TIPS

FEEDER DIET: Suet, black-oil and hulled sunflower seeds, peanuts, mealworms. **FEEDER TYPES**: Suet cages. **FEEDER BEHAVIOR**: Hammers its bill against the suet to dislodge bite-size pieces. Other birds may initially fly away if startled by its arrival.

COMPARE TO SIMILAR SPECIES: Size and distinctive head markings contrast with those of other woodpeckers.

DID YOU KNOW? Pileated Woodpeckers rarely reuse the same nest cavity. This allows many other cavity-nesting birds, many of which are not able to drill their own cavities, to use the hole for nests in future years.

J F M A M J J A S O N D

① **GREEN HERON.** *Butorides virescens.*

SIZE: 17 in.

HABITAT: Wetlands and ponds, sometimes edges of reservoirs and small lakes.

WILD DIET: Mainly small fish. Also, frogs, insects and spiders, small rodents, and aquatic invertebrates.

BEHAVIOR: A solitary hunter at dusk and dawn, usually remaining somewhat secretive during the day. This species is often observed perched motionless on the edge of the water or in the shallows, waiting for prey to approach. Individuals may also rest aboveground in dense tangles of branches. Suburbanites very occasionally observe these birds flying between foraging locations, with somewhat quick, labored wingbeats, head tucked back, and legs outstretched behind.

MIGRATE? Yes.

NESTING: Hidden amid dense cover in the crotch of a tree, usually near wetland habitat. Twigs are used to weave a sturdy bowl. About 1 ft. in diameter.

EGGS: Light blue-green. Length of 1 ½ in. Total of 2-5, occasionally with a second brood.

FEEDER BEHAVIOR: Does not visit feeders.

COMPARE TO SIMILAR SPECIES: Dark green back and head, chestnut-colored chest, yellow legs, and partially yellow bill distinguish from other herons and bitterns. Juveniles are buffier all over with a dark head crown.

DID YOU KNOW? The Green Heron is known for exhibiting remarkable feats of intelligence. It sometimes bait-fishes by finding a piece of bread, an insect, or a colorful object to drop on the water's surface; fish are attracted to the decoy and immediately snatched by the heron. Locations where Green Herons have used bread are also frequented by fishermen; consequently, scientists believe that these clever birds may have learned to bait-fish by direct observation of humans.

J F M A M J J A S O N D

Adults at top and bottom.

Close-up of male at top,
Two males with female at bottom.

① RING-NECKED DUCK. *Aythya collaris.*

SIZE: 17 in.

HABITAT: Wetlands and shallow lakes, ponds. Breeds in wetlands.

WILD DIET: Mostly aquatic vegetation, also aquatic invertebrates and insects.

BEHAVIOR: This species favors the shallows—fully diving beneath the surface as it forages throughout the water column. Compared to many of the dabbling ducks which share their shallow, aquatic habitats, these brief dives enable the Ring-necked Duck to reach vegetation otherwise out of reach for many other species. Sometimes flocks in very large groups, but also may be found in small groups of under a dozen. Mature individuals seem to prefer vegetation to a mixed, omnivorous diet.

MIGRATE? Yes.

NESTING: Nests directly on the water, forming a loose, makeshift bowl of twigs, stems, and grasses atop floating mats of vegetation. About 1 - 1 ½ ft. across.

EGGS: Light brown. Length of 2 in. Total of 6-12.

FEEDER BEHAVIOR: Does not visit feeders.

COMPARE TO SIMILAR SPECIES: Most similar to the Greater and Lesser Scaup (which, it must be noted, tend to frequent larger bodies of water, such as bays), but male's feathery tuft atop the crown, black back, white markings up the side of the chest, and ring across bill are distinctive. Females are best identified by a light ring across the bill and a light eye-ring.

DID YOU KNOW? The Ring-necked Duck is named for the scarcely visible reddish-brown ring around the neck of males; this is typically only observable upon careful inspection at a close distance. In the early days of identification, observers would fire upon birds with shotguns and directly approach any fallen individuals—making finer details, such as the ring about this species' neck, much more visible. With binoculars not widely available before the late 1800s, this was the only manner by which most naturalists could accurately identify many of the birds they encountered.

J F M A M J J A S O N D

④ **LAUGHING GULL.** *Leucophaeus atricilla.*

SIZE: 16 in.

HABITAT: Oceanic coastlines. Also, sometimes in nearby wetlands, lakes, grain fields, or landfills. Usually not observed more than 25 miles from the coast.

WILD DIET: Diverse and adaptable. Includes insects and invertebrates, garbage, food handouts (though this is not recommended), and even roadkill.

BEHAVIOR: Flocks in large groups, sometimes numbering in the thousands. This species may be accompanied by other gull or tern species. Laughing Gulls lead a boisterous and opportunistic livelihood, noisily chattering with their characteristic *ha-ha-ha...* calls and investigating potential food sources. Individuals are often quite bold toward humans in locations where there is regular interaction.

MIGRATE? Yes.

NESTING: Colonial nesters in coastal saltmarshes, on beaches, and on islands. A semi-woven thatching of vegetation is used to constructed a bowl. About 1 ft. across and 1-3 in. deep.

EGGS: Brown or light blue-green, with mottling. Length of 2 in. Total of 2-4.

FEEDER BEHAVIOR: Does not visit feeders.

COMPARE TO SIMILAR SPECIES: Most similar to the Bonaparte's Gull, which shares territory with the Laughing across much of the Atlantic seaboard, and the Franklin's Gull, which passes through the western reaches of its territory during migration. The Bonaparte's shares the black hood during breeding season, but has a far more petite bill and is of smaller size; during nonbreeding season, it has a defined black ear spot rather than the smudging of the Laughing. The Franklin's shares the black hood during breeding season, but has conspicuous white wingtip spotting at this time (rather than black folded wingtips); it retains a partial black hood near the back of the head during nonbreeding season.

DID YOU KNOW? When formalizing this species' scientific name, the Swedish taxonomist Carl Linnaeus mistakenly named it *atricilla* (black-tailed) instead of *atricapilla* (black-haired), a clear error given this bird's black head and white tail—the latter of which is often covered at rest by its black wingtips.

J F M A M J J A S O N D

Nonbreeding adult at top,
Breeding adult at bottom.

Adult at top,
Juvenile at bottom (Photo by Tony Alter / CC BY-SA / Cropped).

③ **COOPER'S HAWK.** *Accipiter cooperii.*

SIZE: 16 in.

HABITAT: Dense or open woods, suburbs.

WILD DIET: Mostly medium-sized birds (e.g., doves, robins, and jays), but also small rodents.

BEHAVIOR: Accustomed to deftly flying through cluttered woodland in search of prey. When pursuing its quarry, individuals will hopscotch among concealed perches before briskly swooping at all manner of angles to secure its catch. Its relatively short wings are extremely well adapted for this agile, close-quarters maneuvering, rather than the long gliding favored by many hawks of open country.

MIGRATE? Partially.

NESTING: Situated in large trees, 25-60 ft. above the ground. Platform composed of sticks, with small indentation in the center for eggs. About 2 ft. across and 1 ft. deep.

EGGS: Very light blue. Length of 2 in. Total of 3-5.

FEEDER BEHAVIOR: Often hunts at feeders, particularly if seed is present on the ground (so as to attract ground-feeding prey birds). After a sequence of attacks, it may take several days for feeder activity to fully return to previous levels.

COMPARE TO SIMILAR SPECIES: Longer tail, head-cap markings, coloration, and habitat selection usually differentiate from Red-tailed and Red-shouldered Hawks. Defined dark cap on top of head, as well as often larger size, differentiate adults from adult Sharp-shinned Hawks. Larger size and more defined, mocha-brown markings on chest differentiate juveniles from juvenile Sharp-shinned Hawks.

DID YOU KNOW? Given their penchant for weaving among trees beneath the forest canopy, as many as one-third of all individuals suffer fractures of bones in the chest at some point in their lives, though these wounds tend to recalcify in time.

J F M A M J J A S O N D

115

① **AMERICAN COOT.** *Fulica americana.*

SIZE: 16 in.

HABITAT: Shorelines of lakes, ponds, and wetlands. Typically found in areas of somewhat dense aquatic vegetation.

WILD DIET: Mostly aquatic vegetation, but sometimes aquatic invertebrates, small fish, and amphibians.

BEHAVIOR: These aquatic, chicken-like birds are often found in flocks of at least a dozen, sometimes many more, and congregate in the shallows on bodies of water of varying size. Foraging is conducted by shallow dives, dabbling, or even standing near the shore or in a few inches of water, plucking algae and grasses with its stubby bill. The coot's lobed toes increase its swimming proficiency, while also preserving its ability to navigate effectively on dry land. Small wings relative to body weight result in a high degree of wing-loading; this is further evidenced by slow, awkward flights and long, running takeoffs. Individuals may loosely associate with some species of ducks.

MIGRATE? Yes.

NESTING: Builds nest overwater on a floating platform of existing aquatic vegetation, weaving together nearby reeds and grasses. About 1 ft. across. Hens often lay eggs in nests of other coots or even those of ducks.

EGGS: Shades of gray or light brown, with dark speckling. Length of 2 in. Total of 5-12, sometimes with a second brood.

FEEDER BEHAVIOR: Does not visit feeders.

COMPARE TO SIMILAR SPECIES: Short, white bill and squat silhouette are very distinctive.

DID YOU KNOW? The American Coot is the namesake for the Toledo Mud Hens, a long-standing Minor League Baseball team. The original ballpark built near the city of Toledo, Ohio was adjacent to vast wetlands inhabited by flocks of coots, and the locals have taken to embracing this unique avian moniker ever since.

J F M A M J J A S O N D

Adults at top, center, and bottom.

Breeding male at top,
Female at bottom.

① **RUDDY DUCK.** *Oxyura jamaicensis.*

SIZE: 15 in.

HABITAT: Wetlands, lakes, ponds, and bays.

WILD DIET: Aquatic invertebrates, insects, and vegetation.

BEHAVIOR: A diving duck, this species usually forages in the shallows, surfacing with a mouthful of water and straining out its prey through small openings in the bill. This straining process is especially critical for a species which derives much of its food from the muddy, clouded benthos of shallow wetlands and ponds. The Ruddy Duck is a quick flyer, but not particularly nimble in the air, preferring to instead stay on the water and dive below if a predator approaches—the general approach for many diving ducks. Newborn young are unusually precocial, and often receive minimal guidance from their parents as they acclimate to the surrounding environment. Does not usually flock with other duck species.

MIGRATE? Yes.

NESTING: Nest is constructed just above water level in wetlands, and woven among the aquatic reeds and cattails. This takes the form of a cup or bowl, and is often crowned with a woven canopy roof of grasses. Usually less than 1 ft. across.

EGGS: Off-white. Length of 2 ½ in. Total of 5-11, sometimes with a second brood.

FEEDER BEHAVIOR: Does not visit feeders.

COMPARE TO SIMILAR SPECIES: Breeding male's bright blue bill (dark gray or black in fall and winter), large white cheek patch, and often upturned tail are characteristic. Female is best identified by small size, in addition to its distinctive markings.

DID YOU KNOW? Ruddy Ducks lay the largest eggs relative to body size of any duck in the world. This allows hatchlings to be quickly capable of functioning on their own—a critical proposition for such a diminutive species of waterfowl.

J F M A M J J A S O N D

119

③ **FISH CROW.** *Corvus ossifragus.*

SIZE: 15 in.

HABITAT: Coastlines of oceans, lakes, rivers, and wetlands. Sometimes observed in nearby urban and suburban areas, also grain fields and landfills.

WILD DIET: Crabs, shrimp, bird eggs and hatchlings, sometimes fish. In terrestrial locations, also the following: grains, fruits, reptiles and amphibians, garbage.

BEHAVIOR: Most often associated with the various bodies of water they are known to frequent, the Fish Crow is an opportunistic feeder both in terms of habitat and dietary selection. This species is commonly observed stealing the eggs and fledglings of other birds. Like most corvids (i.e., the family of jays, crows, ravens, etc.), this species possesses an unusual degree of intelligence.

MIGRATE? Mostly.

NESTING: Often nests near treetops. Large bowl of sticks, twigs. About 2 ft. wide.

EGGS: Light blue-green, with dark speckling. Length of 1 ½ in. Total of 3-5.

BIRD FEEDING TIPS

FEEDER DIET: Black-oil and hulled sunflower seeds, suet, oats, cracked corn, peanuts and peanut hearts, millet, milo, fruit. **FEEDER TYPES**: Ground, platforms. **FEEDER BEHAVIOR**: Does not usually visit feeders, but may be present if near a known habitat. Large size and bold attitude may intimidate some birds upon arrival.

COMPARE TO SIMILAR SPECIES: Very similar to American Crow, but slightly smaller (though this is not a reliable indicator) and far more habitat-specific. Best distinguished by voice; the American Crow emits a well-known, bellowing *caw-caw*, while the Fish Crow gives a very nasal *aw-aw* or *uh-uh*.

DID YOU KNOW? Some Fish Crows have been known to wait outside fast food restaurants each day at the time when garbage is taken out, then scavenge for scraps, take the resulting foodstuffs to nearby puddles and birdbaths, and return several hours later once the meal has been better softened for consumption.

J F M A M J J A S O N D

Adult at top (Photo by Peter W. Chen / CC BY-SA),
Adult at bottom (Photo by Chuck Homler / CC BY-SA / Cropped).

Breeding adult at top left,
Nonbreeding adult at top right,
Nonbreeding adult in flght at bottom (Photo by Mike Baird / CC BY-SA / Cropped).

① **WILLET.** *Tringa semipalmata.*

SIZE: 15 in.

HABITAT: Variety of habitats along oceanic coastlines, including open beaches, sheltered inlets, and tidal zones. During migration, observable in wetlands and flooded fields, as well as on coastlines of larger bodies of water.

WILD DIET: Small crabs, clams, insects (e.g., beetles and insect larvae) and spiders, small fish.

BEHAVIOR: An adaptable forager, this species pursues its prey by a variety of means: methodically walking through the shallows and occasionally pecking throughout the water column, chasing fish and water spiders up to breast-deep, or probing in muddier substrates for invertebrates submerged beneath the visible surface. Except on more crowded wintering grounds, this bird is typically seen on a solitary basis or in lone pairs. So-named for its screechy *pill-will-willet* call.

MIGRATE? Yes.

NESTING: In eastern U.S., typically nests on oceanic shorelines amid the fringes of saltmarshes or atop sand dunes. A shallow bowl of dry grasses and reeds is constructed on the ground. About 6 in. across.

EGGS: Off-white to yellow-brown, with dark mottling. Length of 2 in. Total of 3-4.

FEEDER BEHAVIOR: Does not visit feeders.

COMPARE TO SIMILAR SPECIES: Most similar to Greater and Lesser Yellowlegs, though both of these species lack the distinctive white and black barring across the Willet's wing in flight, have noticeably yellow legs (as the common names would suggest, rather than the pale legs of the Willet), and slightly smaller heads.

DID YOU KNOW? Willets are known to mate for life, returning to the same breeding site each year—a somewhat unusual practice among shorebirds.

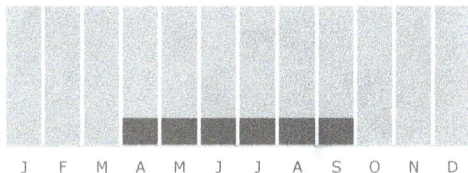

J F M A M J J A S O N D

② BUFFLEHEAD. *Bucephala albeola.*

SIZE: 14 in.

HABITAT: Harbors and bays of oceans and the Great Lakes. Sometimes lakes and ponds during migration, and especially during breeding season.

WILD DIET: Almost entirely aquatic invertebrates and insects.

BEHAVIOR: The smallest diving duck in North America, this species dives repeatedly below the surface for intervals of less than a half-minute, and to depths of up to 20 feet. It must take these foraging dives persistently throughout the day in order to sustain its unusually high metabolism. Like other diving ducks, this species is not usually observed walking on land, with the feet set behind each individual's center of mass to best allow for efficient underwater paddling. Furthermore, its diminutive size is specifically adapted to fill a unique ecological niche. While individuals forage in habitats frequented by other diving ducks, they nest almost entirely in cavities left by Northern Flickers, rather than the larger hollows left by Pileated Woodpeckers (which are subject to fierce competition from other, larger cavity-nesting ducks).

MIGRATE? Yes.

NESTING: Breeds in wooded areas near lakes and ponds. Nests in cavities left by Northern Flickers, or in nest boxes. Lined with feathers. Entrance usually less than 4 in. wide.

EGGS: Shiny, milky white. Length of 2 in. Total of 6-12.

FEEDER BEHAVIOR: Does not visit feeders, but sometimes uses nest boxes.

COMPARE TO SIMILAR SPECIES: White chest and belly distinguish males from Hooded Merganser males, and females have a distinctive white mark behind the eye.

DID YOU KNOW? The seemingly large head of this duck led early observers to give it the name of "buffalo head," the portmanteau of which remains this species' common name today. Similarly, the genus name is derived from the Ancient Greek *Bucephalus*, or "ox-headed," which was also the given name of Alexander the Great's valorous, well-renowned warhorse.

J F M A M J J A S O N D

Male at top (Photo by Mike Pazzani / CC BY-SA / Cropped),
Females at bottom.

Male at top,
Female at bottom (Photo by Mike Pazzani / CC BY-SA).

① GREEN-WINGED TEAL. *Anas carolinensis.*

SIZE: 14 in.

HABITAT: Wetlands, ponds, mudflats, and sometimes agricultural fields.

WILD DIET: Mostly aquatic vegetation, also agricultural waste grains and aquatic invertebrates.

BEHAVIOR: A dabbling duck, this species periodically upends itself as it forages just below the water's surface, though mudflats are another favored foraging site. The Green-winged Teal is the smallest dabbling duck in North America, and is able to adapt to a variety of wetland habitats.

MIGRATE? Yes.

NESTING: Selects a site near, but not usually adjacent to, wetlands. A shallow, small depression is scraped into the grass and lined with twigs, grasses, and feathers. About 6 in. across.

EGGS: Off-white. Length of 2 in. Total of 7-12.

FEEDER BEHAVIOR: Does not visit feeders.

COMPARE TO SIMILAR SPECIES: Male is best identified by its horizontal green facial patch and silvery body. Females lack pale coloration at the base of the bill, which is notably found in female Blue-winged Teals. Females also have a pale, white stripe beneath the tail. Wholly dark-gray bill and diminutive size help to differentiate females from those of other, larger species (such as the common Mallard).

DID YOU KNOW? The story of the Green-winged Teal is often all about the debates surrounding its subspecies. The Eurasian Teal is considered by some to be a separate species entirely, and by others to be conspecific; rare vagrants are sometimes observed on the Atlantic coast, with males best identified by their horizontal white marking along the upper folded wing. The Aleutian Islands subspecies, meanwhile, is unusual in that it has adapted to live year-round in its habitat, despite the inhospitable winter conditions; some of these birds feed on beaches during winter, possibly mimicking a natural preference for mudflats.

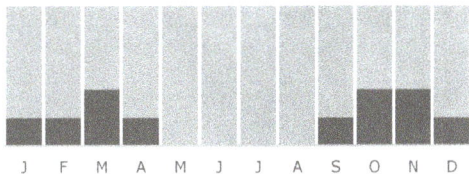

J F M A M J J A S O N D

① COMMON TERN. *Sterna hirundo.*

SIZE: 14 in.

HABITAT: Coastlines of oceans or large inland bodies of water (e.g., Great Lakes). Rare elsewhere during migration, or otherwise.

WILD DIET: Mostly small fish. Sometimes small squid, shrimp, and crabs.

BEHAVIOR: Found unaccompanied or in flocks, this tern forages by swooping from heights of less than 25 feet for prey spotted near the surface of the water below. This species usually forages over open water within 10 miles of coastlines, and is known to rest on boats between hunting sessions if there is no nearby beach or pier. Like many open-water birds of this variety, this species may follow groups of predatory fish—such as tuna or dolphins—and profit from shoals of prey fish being flushed to the surface.

MIGRATE? Yes.

NESTING: Colonial nester. Usually selects a beach, where a small depression is excavated. Nest is lined with twigs, grasses, or small stones. About 6-9 in. across.

EGGS: Blue-green or brown, with dark mottling. Length of 2 in. Total of 2-3, occasionally with a second brood.

FEEDER BEHAVIOR: Does not visit feeders.

COMPARE TO SIMILAR SPECIES: Straight, pointed bill and streamlined profile distinguish from small gulls. This species is very similar to the Forster's Tern in both size and coloration. Differences include the following: the Common has gray upperwing coloration, while the Forster's has white; the Common has darker wingtips when viewed at rest, while on the Forster's these are light gray or whitish; and the Common possesses a black nape in fall and winter, while Forster's has a large black spot over the eye. In addition, the Arctic Tern is similar to the Common, but is only present north of NJ and rare inland; it also has a shorter bill and legs.

DID YOU KNOW? Owing to the precarious waterfront position of this species' nests, mothers are able to distinguish their eggs from those of other nearby nests, even when swept a short distance away.

J F M A M J J A S O N D

Adult in breeding plumage at top,
Adults in nonbreeding plumage at bottom.

Breeding adults at top,
Nonbreeding adult at bottom.

① **HORNED GREBE.** *Podiceps auritus.*

SIZE: 14 in.

HABITAT: Coastlines of oceans and lakes. Also, rivers, ponds, and wetlands.

WILD DIET: Aquatic invertebrates, small fish, and insects.

BEHAVIOR: Like other grebes, this species is known for its extraordinary aptitude for swimming and diving—owing to large, webbed feet located well behind the center of gravity. Consequently, individuals are most often observed on the water, and rarely on land. May launch submerged attacks on small ducks during the breeding season to defend its territory. Found by itself or in very small groups in both the shallows and a few hundred yards offshore in open water, at depths of up to 50 to 80 feet.

MIGRATE? Yes.

NESTING: Anchored to floating aquatic vegetation, and takes the approximate shape of a platform. Constructed of twigs and stems. Less than 8 in. wide.

EGGS: Off-white to brown. Length of 1 ½ - 2 in. Total of 3-6, occasionally with a second brood.

FEEDER BEHAVIOR: Does not visit feeders.

COMPARE TO SIMILAR SPECIES: Breeding adults are highly distinctive. Nonbreeding adults are slightly larger than the similar nonbreeding Eared Grebe, which is less common and more westerly in its range; additional differences include the Horned's oblong (rather than somewhat round or square) head, and more complete white coloration along the side of the head and neck.

DID YOU KNOW? The introduction of certain fish species for sport, such as rainbow trout (also known as steelhead) across North America, has led to diminishing food supplies for grebes, which have suffered declines in the past half-century. Grebes are generally also sensitive to salinity and toxin levels in their habitats, which can affect the availability of food and nesting materials.

J F M A M J J A S O N D

② **PIED-BILLED GREBE.** *Podilymbus podiceps.*

SIZE: 14 in.

HABITAT: Wetlands, ponds, lakes, calmer sections of rivers.

WILD DIET: Mostly crustaceans and small fish (up to 6 in. long). Also, other aquatic invertebrates, insects, and amphibians.

BEHAVIOR: Active divers, grebes are known for their exceptional maneuverability while swimming underwater—on account of large, webbed feet located behind the center of gravity. As a result of this adaptation, individuals tend to be quite ungainly on land and are almost always observed in the water. With graceful, arced leaps, these birds frequently dive below the surface and can reach depths of up to 50 feet repeatedly throughout the day. When surfacing with a small fish, the grebe tosses and spins the catch in its bill, before swallowing it headfirst. Often found in small groups or by themselves, scattered across the surface of the water.

MIGRATE? Yes.

NESTING: Anchored to floating aquatic vegetation, and takes the approximate shape of a platform. Constructed of twigs and stems. Less than 6 in. wide.

EGGS: White. Length of 1 ½ - 2 in. Total of 3-8, sometimes with a second brood.

FEEDER BEHAVIOR: Does not visit feeders.

COMPARE TO SIMILAR SPECIES: Very small size among the waterfowl, and distinctively small and stubby bill relative to other species.

DID YOU KNOW? Grebes, including the Pied-billed, are well-known for consuming their own feathers, which may help with the following: protecting the stomach from indigestible bones or shells, preventing these items from passing to the intestines, or allowing for these indigestible items to be more easily packaged as pellets for regurgitation. In some grebes, the stomach has been observed to be up to half-full with feathered contents.

J F M A M J J A S O N D

132

Breeding adult with juvenile at top,
Nonbreeding adult at bottom.

Adult resting in nonbreeding plumage at top,
Adults in breeding plumage at bottom.

② **FORSTER'S TERN.** *Sterna forsteri.*

SIZE: 14 in.

HABITAT: Coastlines of oceans, lakes, and rivers. Also, (usually expansive) wetlands.

WILD DIET: Mostly small fish (e.g., minnows, sunfish, perch, sardines). Occasionally, flying insects.

BEHAVIOR: A tern which breeds in wetlands during the spring and summer, this species is subsequently found in a wide variety of habitats throughout the balance of the year. When migrating and wintering, larger bodies of water are often inhabited. Like many terns, this species will often fly 15 to 30 feet above the water's surface, scanning for prey before plunge-diving in pursuit; however, unlike many of its relatives, this tern also has a penchant for perching over the water on dock pilings, fencing, or wires and waiting for suitable prey to swim nearby.

MIGRATE? Yes.

NESTING: Colonial nester. Selects a location at ground level amid dense wetland vegetation or even atop floating vegetation. May be a shallow depression or well-defined cup, usually lined with grasses. About 6-9 in. across.

EGGS: Light brown, with dark mottling, speckling. Length of 1 ½ in. Total of 2-4.

FEEDER BEHAVIOR: Does not visit feeders.

COMPARE TO SIMILAR SPECIES: Straight, pointed bill and streamlined profile distinguish from small gulls. This species is very similar to the Forster's Tern in both size and coloration. Differences include the following: the Common has gray upperwing coloration, while the Forster's has silvery white; the Common has darker folded rear wingtips when viewed at rest, while on the Forster's these are light gray or whiteish; and the Common possesses a black nape in fall and winter, while the Forster's instead has a large black spot over the eye.

DID YOU KNOW? Forster's Terns are aggressive in defense of their nests, and some other wetland breeders, such as ducks, grebes, and blackbirds, have been known to nest nearby in order to benefit from the resultant sphere of protection.

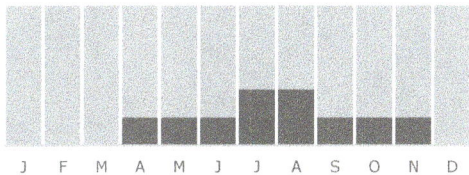

J F M A M J J A S O N D

② **BOAT-TAILED GRACKLE.** *Quiscalus major.*

SIZE: 14 in.

HABITAT: Mostly wetlands, sometimes urban areas and fields. Rarely far from saltwater, except in Peninsular Florida.

WILD DIET: Grains, fruits, insects and spiders, worms, reptiles and amphibians, small fish, and garbage.

BEHAVIOR: These birds are perhaps best known for their large populations in and around saltwater wetlands: foraging by probing in the sand, soil, or shallow water for food items. Most individuals will not move more than 25 miles from their birthplace over a lifetime, and will remain within 10 to 25 miles of the oceanic coast. May loosely flock with the Great-tailed Grackle where their ranges overlap.

MIGRATE? No.

NESTING: Located a few feet aboveground in a bush, amid dense wetland vegetation. Occasionally in trees. The nest is a tight cup, woven with twigs and grasses. About 8 in. across.

EGGS: Light brown to light blue-green, with muddy splotches. Length of 1 ½ in. Total of 1-5, with 1-2 broods.

BIRD FEEDING TIPS

FEEDER DIET: Black-oil and hulled sunflower seeds, cracked corn, peanut hearts, millet, safflower seed. **FEEDER TYPES**: Ground, platforms. **FEEDER BEHAVIOR**: Can accumulate in flocks, and aggressive behavior may frighten away other bird species.

COMPARE TO SIMILAR SPECIES: Dark eye distinguishes from the Great-tailed Grackle in TX and LA, in addition to habitat (Boat-taileds rarely wander far from water) and smaller size. Larger with longer tail than the Common Grackle.

DID YOU KNOW? This grackle species possesses loads of intelligence, with individuals frequently spotted retrieving scraps of human food and briefly submerging them in water for easier, less inhibited consumption.

J F M A M J J A S O N D

Male at top,
Female at bottom.

Adult at top,
Adults in flight at bottom.

④ **ROCK DOVE (or ROCK PIGEON).**
Columba livia.

SIZE: 13 in.
HABITAT: Urban areas.
WILD DIET: Grains, seeds, berries, and garbage.
BEHAVIOR: Forages on the ground, often in flocks of at least several dozen. Also loiters in parks if there is a consistent source of human-supplied food. While walking along, this species repeatedly nods its head forward, which provides a steadier field of vision by counterbalancing its choppy gait. Large flocks are often observed perched on telephone wires, ledges of buildings, or billboards.
MIGRATE? No.
NESTING: In urban areas, nests in crevices or on ledges of buildings, particularly where there is some overhead shelter. Small platform, constructed with sticks and vegetation. Over time, may grow in size with the accumulated feces of past nesting generations.
EGGS: White. Length of 1 ½ in. Total of 2. Usually raises 3-4 broods each year, but may raise up to 6.

BIRD FEEDING TIPS

FEEDER DIET: Black-oil and hulled sunflower seeds, cracked corn, peanut hearts, millet, safflower seed. **FEEDER TYPES**: Ground, platforms, hoppers. **FEEDER BEHAVIOR**: Most likely to visit if feeders are situated near urban centers, bridges, or overpasses.

COMPARE TO SIMILAR SPECIES: Similar in shape and silhouette to Mourning Dove, but note clear difference in coloration and markings.

DID YOU KNOW? Due to their characteristic homing abilities, domesticated pigeons have long been used to convey messages to distant locations. Rock Doves, in particular, have been used to carry such things as postal messages and wartime communications over distances spanning hundreds—and even thousands—of miles.

J F M A M J J A S O N D

139

② GREATER YELLOWLEGS. *Tringa melanoleuca.*

SIZE: 13 in.

HABITAT: Wetlands, mudflats, flooded fields; also, edges of streams, ponds, reservoirs, lakes.

WILD DIET: Aquatic insects and invertebrates, sometimes fish and small frogs.

BEHAVIOR: Usually observed foraging solitarily, with a slight preference for deeper portions of shallows compared to other shorebirds. Wades through the water or walks across mudflats with a peculiar, high-stepping motion. Known for striking its prey with a quick downward peck or by repeated probing motions: particularly when foraging in more turbid, or opaque, waters. Rather unusually for a shorebird, males may be observed standing sentry over their nesting territories from elevated positions in the treetops, most often during the breeding season.

MIGRATE? Yes.

NESTING: Selects a concealed location amid the dense vegetation at the edges of wetlands. Digs a light scrape in the moss or soil. Up to 6 in. across.

EGGS: Light brown with heavy dark mottling. Length of 2 in. Total of 3-4.

FEEDER BEHAVIOR: Does not visit feeders.

COMPARE TO SIMILAR SPECIES: Large size and conspicuous, bright yellow legs distinguish from most other shorebird species. Lesser Yellowlegs is very similar, but stands a few inches shorter, and has a bill approximately the length of its head (compared to that of the Greater, which is at least one-and-a-half times the length of its head). Also, the bill of the Greater is slightly upturned at the end, though this can be difficult to spot in the field.

DID YOU KNOW? Despite its remarkable similarity with the Lesser Yellowlegs, this species is actually more closely related to the gray-legged Willet. All three species are members of the *Tringa* genus, which was named for an antiquitous shorebird originally described by the Greek polymath Aristotle.

J F M A M J J A S O N D

Breeding adult at top,
Nonbreeding adult at bottom.

Male at top,
Female at bottom (Notice presence of chestnut breast coloration).

② **BELTED KINGFISHER.** *Megaceryle alcyon.*

SIZE: 13 in.

HABITAT: Variety of bodies of water, including bays, lakes, rivers, and ponds. Prefers to hunt over calm, clearer water whenever available.

WILD DIET: Mostly small fish (e.g., trout, perch, sunfish, sticklebacks), sometimes crayfish, snails, amphibians, insects, and small mammals.

BEHAVIOR: This species is often found on the fringes of local ponds and streams, perched atop a post, branch, or wire overlooking the water. When prey is spotted, the kingfisher flies near the targeted location, often hovers momentarily on flapping wings, and plunge-dives bill-first to collect its meal. The catch is then consumed headfirst from a nearby perch. As the kingfisher flies around its habitat, it commonly emits a series of characteristic, rattling calls, which provide a telltale indicator of its nearby presence.

MIGRATE? Partially.

NESTING: Digs a long, hidden burrow into a vertical or steeply sloped earthen bank. About 3-8 ft. deep with an enlarged, elevated nest chamber at the terminus.

EGGS: Bright white. Length of 1 ½ in. Total of 4-8, sometimes with a second brood.

FEEDER BEHAVIOR: Does not visit feeders.

COMPARE TO SIMILAR SPECIES: Very distinctive, there are few birds which resemble this species. In S Texas, the larger Ringed Kingfisher has a more sizable bill and females have a fully orange-red chest and belly; also in S Texas, the smaller Green Kingfisher possesses a dark green cast and lacks the spiky crest of Belted.

DID YOU KNOW? The tricks of the Belted Kingfisher's trade are carefully guarded and passed from generation to generation. Parents teach their young to hunt by dropping dead prey fish in the water for retrieval, allowing the young an opportunity to wet their bills before heading off on their own.

J F M A M J J A S O N D

⑤ **COMMON GRACKLE.** *Quiscalus quiscula.*

SIZE: 12 in.

HABITAT: Open woods, wetlands, fields, and suburbs.

WILD DIET: Seeds, grains, insects and spiders, frogs, eggs, mice, and small birds.

BEHAVIOR: Frequently forages across lawns and fields, and perches in shrubs or atop marsh grasses. Roosts high in trees. When flying in search of another location to scavenge, this species may emit a deep *chek* sound; the long, flowing tail with a diamond-like extension is characteristic of this species and highly recognizable.

MIGRATE? Mostly.

NESTING: In conifers, well above the ground. Often near wetland habitats. Cup-shaped, constructed of grasses and twigs. Up to 12 in. across, and 8 in. tall.

EGGS: Shades of blue or blue-green, with dark mottling. Length of 1 in. Total of 3-6, occasionally with a second brood.

BIRD FEEDING TIPS

FEEDER DIET: Black-oil and hulled sunflower seeds, suet, safflower seed, cracked corn, peanuts and peanut hearts, oats, millet, milo, fruit. **FEEDER TYPES**: Ground, platforms, hoppers. **FEEDER BEHAVIOR**: Can dominate feeders due to their size and attitudes. Often observed foraging on ground, or briefly perching on bark to feed on suet.

COMPARE TO SIMILAR SPECIES: Long tail with diamond-like attachment is largely distinctive among blackbirds of this size. In addition, the European Starling is smaller, has somewhat different markings, and lacks a relatively long tail.

DID YOU KNOW? The flocking tendency and resourcefulness of this species, along with its preference for seeds and grains, has resulted in millions of dollars' worth of damage to agricultural crops, especially corn.

J F M A M J J A S O N D

Male at top,
Female at bottom (Photo by Bob Peterson / CC BY-SA / Cropped).

Adult at left,
Juvenile at right.

② SHARP-SHINNED HAWK. *Accipiter striatus.*

SIZE: 12 in.

HABITAT: Dense woods, sometimes wooded suburbs.

WILD DIET: Mostly small to medium-sized songbirds. Rarely, small rodents.

BEHAVIOR: Selects hidden perches at a variety of heights, ambushing prey with quick and stealthy approaches. Often flies nimbly through dense thickets and forest understories when hunting, requiring split-second reflexes and precise, acrobatic movements. As such, this hawk is a member of the accipiters (along with the closely related Cooper's Hawk), which tend to feature short, rounded wings and long, rudder-like tails as express adaptations for this hunting technique.

MIGRATE? Yes.

NESTING: Usually in conifers, well above the ground. Near the top of tree, but beneath the forest canopy. Platform-shaped and constructed with twigs. About 18 in. across and 4 in. deep.

EGGS: Off-white, with variety of bright splotches. Length of 1 ½ in. Total of 4-6.

FEEDER BEHAVIOR: Sometimes hunts at feeders, but less frequently than the Cooper's Hawk.

COMPARE TO SIMILAR SPECIES: Adults are superficially similar to the Cooper's Hawk, but smaller size, lack of well-defined dark cap on head, and habitat choice are often helpful differences. Juveniles are separated from juvenile Cooper's by less-defined, splotchier, and tawnier chest markings.

DID YOU KNOW? Though one of the more secretive hawks found in North America, this species spectacularly travels en masse during migration, sometimes even overwhelming experienced hawk-watchers. As many as 10,000 individuals have been counted in a single day in some locations—the most productive of which tend to be situated along prominent coastlines or mountain ridges.

J F M A M J J A S O N D

③ **NORTHERN FLICKER.** *Colaptes auratus.*

SIZE: 12 in.

HABITAT: Open woods, fields, and suburbs.

WILD DIET: Mostly insects and spiders (in particular, ants). Also, seeds and berries.

BEHAVIOR: These uniquely patterned woodpeckers are the only species of their kind which routinely feeds on the ground. Ant hills are often sought, and this species' long, nimble tongue is able to extend several inches from its bill to collect larvae and mature ants alike. If present in agricultural pastures, this bird may also hammer apart cow dung in order to feast on any insects present inside.

MIGRATE? Partially.

NESTING: Excavated holes in dead tree trunks or large branches. May be reused from other species. Exterior hole is about 3-4 in. in diameter, and cavity is over 1 ft. deep.

EGGS: White. Length of 1 in. Total of 5-6, sometimes with a second brood.

BIRD FEEDING TIPS

FEEDER DIET: Suet, black-oil and hulled sunflower seeds, safflower seed, cracked corn, peanuts and peanut hearts, millet. **FEEDER TYPES**: Suet cages, ground, platforms, hoppers. **FEEDER BEHAVIOR**: Less common at feeders, but usually observed consuming suet from a cage, or scavenging on the ground.

COMPARE TO SIMILAR SPECIES: Coloration and spotted patterning are distinctive among woodpeckers. Much stouter, thicker neck than doves or robins.

DID YOU KNOW? During the breeding season, dueling males may engage in a bill-sparring match which roughly resembles the Olympic sport of fencing. The prospective female watches from a safe distance—awaiting the winner and soon-to-be mate.

J F M A M J J A S O N D

Adults at top and bottom.

Breeding adult at top,
Nonbreeding adult at bottom.

① **LESSER YELLOWLEGS.** *Tringa flavipes.*

SIZE: 12 in.

HABITAT: Wetlands, mudflats, flooded fields; also, edges of streams, ponds, reservoirs, and lakes.

WILD DIET: Aquatic insects and invertebrates, sometimes fish and small frogs.

BEHAVIOR: Stalks through the shallows of its wetland habitat, occasionally increasing pace or pecking beneath the surface when prey is spotted. Like the Greater Yellowlegs, it also walks with a high-stepping gait and may wade up to its chest while foraging. This allows for individuals to exploit sections of wetland unsuitable for smaller shorebirds, such as Spotted or Least Sandpipers. When foraging, usually present by itself or in very small, scattered numbers. Hatchlings are precocious, leaving the nest within hours and effectively presenting a model of self-sufficiency.

MIGRATE? Yes.

NESTING: Well-concealed locations in the vicinity of its typical wetland habitat, often amid dense vegetation or debris. Digs a light scrape in the moss or soil. About 3-4 in. across.

EGGS: Light brown with heavy dark mottling. Length of 1 ½ - 2 in. Total of 3-4.

FEEDER BEHAVIOR: Does not visit feeders.

COMPARE TO SIMILAR SPECIES: Medium-large size and conspicuous, bright yellow legs distinguish from most other shorebird species. Greater Yellowlegs is very similar, but stands a few inches taller, and has a bill at least one-and-a-half times the length of its head (compared to that of the Lesser, which is about the length of its head).

DID YOU KNOW? When flushed, this wary shorebird usually gives a one- or two-note squeaking call, rather than the more forceful three- or four-note call of the Greater Yellowlegs. To better recall this difference, consider that the Lesser Yellowlegs gives a "lesser" number of notes.

J F M A M J J A S O N D

151

⑤ MOURNING DOVE. *Zenaida macroura.*

SIZE: 12 in.

HABITAT: Open woods, fields, suburbs, roadsides.

WILD DIET: Various seeds.

BEHAVIOR: Often observed perching on wires, fences, roofs, and in trees, while repeatedly *hooing* with its signature, melancholy call. Pecks for food on the ground, and is not an overly picky eater. To accompany its voracious appetite for seeds, this species swallows fine rocks or sands to aid in digestion. Occasionally may be observed sunning itself on the ground, with wings and tail splayed out.

MIGRATE? Partially.

NESTING: Hidden among tree branches, in shrubs, on the ground, or in artificial objects such as eaves and gutters. Cup-shaped, and constructed with conifer needles, grasses, and small sticks. About 8 in. across.

EGGS: White. Length of 1 in. Total of 2. Usually raises 2-3 broods each year, but may raise up to 6.

BIRD FEEDING TIPS

FEEDER DIET: Black-oil and hulled sunflower seeds, safflower seed, cracked corn, peanut hearts, millet, oats, nyjer, milo. **FEEDER TYPES**: Ground, platforms, hoppers. **FEEDER BEHAVIOR**: May rest or forage beneath feeders. Common prey for feeder-raiding Cooper's Hawks, and sometimes Sharp-shinned or even Red-shouldered Hawks.

COMPARE TO SIMILAR SPECIES: Much paler than Rock Doves, and usually found in less urban areas. Tapered, feathered tails are easily observable when perching, which are very different from the more rectangular tails of Sharp-shinned Hawks and American Kestrels, not to mention many other visual differences.

DID YOU KNOW? Occasionally called turtle doves, these birds are anything but slow in flight—reaching speeds of up to 55 mph as they whistle through the air.

J F M A M J J A S O N D

Adult on ground at top,
Adult perched on wire at bottom (Photo by Heide Couch / CC BY-SA / Cropped).

Breeding adult at top (Photo by Dick Daniels / CC BY-SA / Cropped),
Nonbreeding Long-billed adult inset,
Nonbreeding adult at bottom (Photo by Dick Daniels / CC BY-SA).

① **SHORT-BILLED DOWITCHER.**

Limnodromus griseus.

SIZE: 11 in.

HABITAT: During migration, mudflats, wetlands, flooded fields, ponds, and lakes. When wintering, prefers saltwater or brackish tidal zones along the oceanic coast.

WILD DIET: Aquatic insects and insect larvae, aquatic invertebrates (e.g., snails, crabs).

BEHAVIOR: Prefers the muddy shallows, where it can easily probe the water for prey with the lower half of its bill. This species is well known for the back-and-forth motion of its bill in the substrate, rather like the needle of a sewing machine. Due to the tactility of its feeding and its superior low-light vision, dowitchers can often be found feeding after dark.

MIGRATE? Yes.

NESTING: Breeds on the southern edge of Canadian and Alaskan tundra. Selects a grassy location near dense vegetation. Cup-shaped, and constructed with dried vegetation. Less than 5-6 in. across.

EGGS: Light brown with dark mottling. Length of 1 ½ in. Total of 4.

FEEDER BEHAVIOR: Does not visit feeders.

COMPARE TO SIMILAR SPECIES: The Long-billed Dowitcher was considered to be conspecific with this species until the mid-20th Century; as such, the two species of North American dowitchers remain possibly the most difficult to separate of all birds mentioned in this guide. The supercilium, or eyebrow arch, of the Long-billed is nearly straight (as opposed to the more distinctly rounded arch of the Short-billed), and the end of the Long-billed's bill lacks the downward curve of the Short-billed. The Long-billed emits a high-pitched flight call of *kweek* or *pweek*, while the Short-billed has a lower, more bubbly *tu tu tu...* in flight.

DID YOU KNOW? Despite the *Long-billed* and *Short-billed* designations for the two dowitcher species, there is plenty of overlap between their known ranges of bill length and, as such, this is not the best indicator for identification.

J F M A M J J A S O N D

① **BROWN THRASHER.** *Toxostoma rufum.*

SIZE: 11 in.

HABITAT: Thickets, edges of woods.

WILD DIET: Mostly insects and spiders; also berries, nuts, and seeds.

BEHAVIOR: These fierce, boldly patterned birds are typically hidden in areas of dense vegetation, scrub, or overgrown thickets. Though this species may occasionally pick berries and nuts from bushes and trees, it is primarily seen foraging on the ground and in leaf litter with a deft sweeping motion of its decurved bill. Well known for its mimicry of a diverse array of sounds. During breeding season, males often claim a territory of up to several acres in size, which may reduce thrasher concentrations in some areas.

MIGRATE? Mostly.

NESTING: Usually low in a protective shrub or tree. Cup-shaped, and constructed with twigs and sticks, as well as other vegetative matter. About 6 in. across.

EGGS: Light brown, blue, or blue-green, with fine brown speckling. Length of 1 in. Total of 2-5. Raises 1-3 broods each year, but usually 2.

BIRD FEEDING TIPS

FEEDER DIET: Black-oil and hulled sunflower seeds, suet, cracked corn, peanut hearts. **FEEDER TYPES**: Ground, platforms. **FEEDER BEHAVIOR**: Seldom visits backyards, given its preference for dense shrub cover, but may sift through fallen seeds and suet crumbs on the ground beneath feeders.

COMPARE TO SIMILAR SPECIES: Larger (with much longer tail) than Wood Thrush. Patterning, long and decurved bill, and long tail otherwise distinct.

DID YOU KNOW? Thrashers pugnaciously defend their nests, even to the point of drawing blood from dogs and humans.

J F M A M J J A S O N D

Adults at top and bottom.

Adults at top and bottom.

⑤ **BLUE JAY.** *Cyanocitta cristata.*

SIZE: 11 in.

HABITAT: Any type of woods, but especially open woods and edges. Also common in all variety of wooded urban and suburban areas.

WILD DIET: Insects and spiders, nuts, grains, and seeds. May scavenge nearly anything else.

BEHAVIOR: Among the most visible of suburban birds, this species is noisy, active, and brightly colored. Jays are relatives of crows and ravens, and consequently possess many highly intelligent traits, such as intricate structuring of social systems, food caching, and accurate mimicry of other birds and animals. The raucous *jeer* of this species may carry for hundreds of yards across quiet sections of habitat.

MIGRATE? Partially.

NESTING: Selects a location amid the thick branches of a tree, about 10-20 ft. above the ground. Cup-shaped, constructed with soft twigs and grasses, and lined with plant roots. About 6-8 in. across, sometimes sprawling larger.

EGGS: Shades of blue to blue-green, with dirty mottling. Length of 1 in. Total of 3-6, sometimes with a second brood.

BIRD FEEDING TIPS

FEEDER DIET: Black-oil and hulled sunflower seeds, suet, safflower seed, mealworms, cracked corn, peanuts and peanut hearts, fruit, millet, milo. **FEEDER TYPES**: Platforms, suet cages, ground, hoppers, tubes. **FEEDER BEHAVIOR**: May yield to other birds when feeder is contested. Does not usually stay for long, unless very familiar with the surroundings.

COMPARE TO SIMILAR SPECIES: Distinct color and patterning for its size.

DID YOU KNOW? Blue Jays often push acorns into the ground during the fall months, saving them for colder days ahead. In fact, it is believed that this habit helped oak trees to recolonize much of North America following the last ice age.

J F M A M J J A S O N D

① **AMERICAN KESTREL.** *Falco sparverius.*

SIZE: 11 in.

HABITAT: Open fields, including rural farmland and overgrown pasture. Occasionally, cities and suburbs.

WILD DIET: Insects (e.g., grasshoppers), small rodents (e.g., voles, mice) and birds, reptiles, and amphibians.

BEHAVIOR: Often observed scanning the ground from a perch, which may be a wire, post, fence, or exposed tree branch. It quickly dives or hovers as it approaches prey, which is usually struck directly on the ground. Upon returning to a perch, the kestrel consumes its prey piecemeal while holding it securely with one talon. Over a dozen catches may be made in a single hour, depending on the size and variety of prey targeted. Fastidious birders may also notice that individual kestrels tend to perfect their own hunting habits and techniques, similar to the behavior sometimes exhibited by the Peregrine Falcon, its much larger relative.

MIGRATE? Partially.

NESTING: Nests in various cavities, which may be old woodpecker hollows, rock crevices, or nooks in corners of buildings. No nest materials are used.

EGGS: Light brown or off-white, with dirty mottling. Length of 1 ½ in. Total of 3-6, occasionally with a second brood.

FEEDER BEHAVIOR: Rarely hunts at feeders.

COMPARE TO SIMILAR SPECIES: Though the size of a Mourning Dove, this species has bright, colorful markings (especially on males, which feature a bright orange chest and upper back) and a distinctive face. These facial markings, as well as their narrow, pointed wings in flight (characteristic of falcons, such as the Peregrine), help to differentiate from the Sharp-shinned Hawk.

DID YOU KNOW? The American Kestrel is the smallest of all North American falconids, and is hunted by all manner of larger falcons, owls, and hawks, even including the diminutive Sharp-shinned Hawk on occasion.

J F M A M J J A S O N D

Male at top (Photo by Greg Hume / CC BY-SA / Cropped),
Female at bottom (Photo by Andrew Dimler / CC BY-SA / Cropped).

Adult at top,
Juvenile at bottom (Photo by K6ka / CC BY-SA / Cropped).

⑤ AMERICAN ROBIN. *Turdus migratorius.*

SIZE: 10 in.

HABITAT: Open woods, parks, suburbs.

WILD DIET: Insects and spiders, worms, berries, and fruits.

BEHAVIOR: Often seen on suburban lawns, darting and pausing as it passes through the grass, and pulling worms from the soil. Particularly active immediately after rainfall (when worms move to the surface) or lawn mowing. Sings its undulating, cheery melodies of chirps for long periods while perched in trees. During colder months, may flock in very large groups to cooperatively search for food sources.

MIGRATE? No.

NESTING: Finds a location with ample leaf cover or protection, typically in trees or in artificial structures such as gutters, eaves, or streetlights. Cup-shaped, and composed of twigs and vegetation. About 6 in. across and 4 in. deep.

EGGS: Bright, light blue. Length of 1 in. Total of 3-5. Usually raises 2 broods each year, but may raise up to 3.

BIRD FEEDING TIPS

FEEDER DIET: Hulled sunflower seeds, suet, safflower seed, mealworms, fruit, peanut hearts. **FEEDER TYPES**: Ground, platforms. **FEEDER BEHAVIOR**: Very rarely visits feeders, but is frequently observable trotting through nearby lawns, gardens, and mulch beds.

COMPARE TO SIMILAR SPECIES: Juvenile could be confused with a Wood Thrush, but orange on chest and dark-colored head remain distinctive. Adults are quite distinctive and familiar.

DID YOU KNOW? The song of the American Robin has long been associated with the coming of spring, at which time males begin to vociferously seek out mates and defend their breeding territories. Emily Dickinson was especially fond of using this species as an allusion to springtime, with her poems ""Hope" is the thing with feathers" and "I dreaded that first robin so" serving as notable examples.

J F M A M J J A S O N D

④ **RED-BELLIED WOODPECKER.**
Melanerpes carolinus.

SIZE: 9 ¾ in.
HABITAT: Various woods, wooded suburbs.
WILD DIET: Insects and spiders, seeds, nuts, fruits and berries.
BEHAVIOR: Like most woodpeckers, this species hops up and down tree trunks in search of food hidden beneath and between pieces of bark, using its sturdily built tail as a brace to facilitate such movements. Individuals are usually observed in a right-side-up position: inspecting, hammering, and then quickly grabbing food with the tongue. Individuals also frequently cache food in knots or crevices of trees.
MIGRATE? No.
NESTING: May select the trunk of a dead tree used in past years, but excavates a new nest cavity each year. Forms an entrance hole about 4 in. across, and a cavity 1 ft. deep.
EGGS: Shades of white. Length of 1 in. Total of 3-5. Usually raises 1-2 broods each year, but occasionally attempts to hatch and raise a third.

BIRD FEEDING TIPS

FEEDER DIET: Suet, black-oil and hulled sunflower seeds, peanuts and peanut hearts, safflower seed, cracked corn, grape jelly, mealworms, fruit, sugar water. **FEEDER TYPES**: Suet cages, tubes, hoppers, platforms, nectar feeders. **FEEDER BEHAVIOR**: Readily takes suet like many other woodpeckers, though may be present at other feeders as well. May assert its dominance and force other birds to scatter when it lands on a feeder.

COMPARE TO SIMILAR SPECIES: Individuals are often confused with Red-headed Woodpeckers, which possess an entirely red head and neck, rather than just a patch on top. Compared to the Northern Flicker, this species is slightly smaller and has different markings and coloration.

DID YOU KNOW? Due to its preference for building a nest cavity in dead trees, the Red-bellied Woodpecker is particularly vulnerable to the clearing of established woodlots and dying stands of forest.

J F M A M J J A S O N D

Adult male feeding (Note that females have a red patch which extends only partway up the back of the neck, and juveniles often have gray coloration on part or all of patch).

Adult at top,
Juvenile at bottom.

③ NORTHERN MOCKINGBIRD.
Mimus polyglottos.

SIZE: 9 ½ in.

HABITAT: Thickets, suburbs, and parks.

WILD DIET: Insects and spiders, worms, fruits (especially berries), and seeds.

BEHAVIOR: This species actively forages for food on the ground with erratic trots and pauses, as well as in shrubbery and in trees. It is perhaps best known for its diverse repertoire of songs, including detailed mimicries of other birds and neighborhood sounds alike. When singing, this species often sits on a high, elevated perch—such as a tree branch, pole, or fence post—and may continue its noisy vocalizations well into the nighttime hours, particularly during the warmer months. Northern Mockingbirds are also known to be among the most aggressive of all birds in the defense of their nests.

MIGRATE? No.

NESTING: Often nests around shoulder-height in trees and shrubs. Cup-shaped, composed mostly of twigs and vegetation. About 6 in. across.

EGGS: Light blue to blue-green, with brown splotches. Length of 1 in. Total of 3-5, with 2-3 broods.

BIRD FEEDING TIPS

FEEDER DIET: Fruit, mealworms, grape jelly, suet, hulled sunflower seeds, peanut hearts. **FEEDER TYPES**: Ground, platforms. **FEEDER BEHAVIOR**: Uncommonly visits feeders, but may be attracted by (preferably, dense) plantings of native berry bushes.

COMPARE TO SIMILAR SPECIES: Much larger than Gray Catbird, and also differs in the following ways: paler in color, with a light underside; has bars of white on the wings; tail is more spread and feathered; and lacks a dark-colored patch atop the head.

DID YOU KNOW? This species was not historically present in large numbers north of Pennsylvania. However, the recent proliferation of multiflora rose has helped this mockingbird species expand its range northward. This decorative bush has white flowers, and is native to east Asia; consequently, it is an invasive species in North America and should not be actively planted in backyards.

J F M A M J J A S O N D

③ **KILLDEER.** *Charadrius vociferus.*

SIZE: 9 ½ in.

HABITAT: Fields, mudflats, wetlands, and beaches.

WILD DIET: Insects (e.g., beetles, flies), small aquatic invertebrates, worms.

BEHAVIOR: A plover of the ball fields, this species is one of the few shorebirds which regularly visits the rural suburbs. Often flocks when feeding, alternatingly running and pausing as each individual intently searches for food. When taking its invertebrate prey, the Killdeer either snaps up the item with its bill or yanks it forcefully from the substrate. Lone members of the flock aerially rove about nearby, seeking as-yet undiscovered feeding sites. Scatters quickly when approached. When flying, emits its characteristic, squeaky *kill-dee-ur* call.

MIGRATE? Mostly. Some birds may remain for the winter, especially in southern NJ.

NESTING: A shallow rut is scraped into the ground, upon which the eggs are laid. Close to 3 in. across.

EGGS: Whitish-tan, with many large black markings. Length of 1 ½ in. Total of 4-7. May raise 1-3 broods each year, but usually raises 2.

FEEDER BEHAVIOR: Does not visit feeders.

COMPARE TO SIMILAR SPECIES: Long, straight legs help to distinguish this as a shorebird; among other shorebirds and plovers, note this species' large size and two black chest rings (compared to the Semipalmated Plover's one).

DID YOU KNOW? During the breeding season, the Killdeer is well known for diverting predators' attention away from its nests by utilizing several notable display tactics. It may use "broken-wing" displays to lure a predator away before taking evasive flight, or alternatively spread its feathers and directly charge the intruder. However, it is best to watch from a safe distance: *never* closely approach bird nests, as this can adversely affect breeding success.

J F M A M J J A S O N D

Adult wading at top,
Adults in flight at bottom (Photo by Magnus Manske / CC BY-SA).

Male at top,
Female at bottom (Photo by Simon Wray / CC BY-SA).

③ HAIRY WOODPECKER. *Dryobates villosus.*

SIZE: 9 ¼ in.

HABITAT: Woods, especially dense, mature woods. Sometimes suburbs and parks.

WILD DIET: Mostly insects and larvae, but also nuts, seeds, and berries.

BEHAVIOR: Feeds by boring holes into tree bark, as well as by prying off slabs of bark with its bill. Often prefers to rest high in mature tree stands, which can make this species difficult to spot. In addition, this species' rapid-fire drilling pattern is among the fastest of all woodpeckers' (about 25 to 30 beats per minute), which can assist with identification once a few species have been compared in the field.

MIGRATE? No.

NESTING: Drills a cavity in a dead or decaying tree. Forms an entrance hole about 2 in. across, with a cavity extending about 1 ft. deep.

EGGS: Shades of white. Length of 1 in. Total of 3-5.

BIRD FEEDING TIPS

FEEDER DIET: Suet, black-oil and hulled sunflower seeds, peanuts and peanut hearts, mealworms, safflower seed. **FEEDER TYPES**: Suet cages, tubes, hoppers, platforms. **FEEDER BEHAVIOR**: May take time to attract, but will often return after first visiting. Mostly eats suet. Can also engage in mild acrobatics on feeders when reaching for seed.

COMPARE TO SIMILAR SPECIES: Nearly identical to Downy Woodpecker, apart from its notably larger average size. Other key differences include a bill which is about as long as the length of its head (rather than smaller), and possession of clean outer white tail feathers (rather than spotted).

DID YOU KNOW? This species may be attracted by the dozens to sections of forest experiencing mass beetle infestations. Though not often witnessed, this spectacle is a wonderful opportunity to observe the Hairy for extended periods.

J   F   M   A   M   J   J   A   S   O   N   D

① LEAST TERN. *Sternula antillarum.*

SIZE: 9 in.

HABITAT: Breeds on coastlines of oceans and lakes, especially semi-sheltered bays and inlets; also, moves up rivers in the central U.S. Winters south of U.S.

WILD DIET: Small fish and crustaceans.

BEHAVIOR The smallest of the North American terns, this species is often conspicuous among seabirds for its diminutive size. Often observed scanning the water as it flies above; upon sighting a school of small fish, it typically plunges to the surface bill-first and quickly takes off with prey in tow, after minimal submersion. Least Terns are capable of quick, nimble flight as they weave and circle about their hunting grounds, navigating with brief flits of the wings.

MIGRATE? Yes.

NESTING: Loose colonial nester. Nest is located on beaches of shorelines or small islands, and consists of a shallow indentation in the substrate. About 6 in. across.

EGGS: Off-white, light brown, or blue, with dark mottling or spotting. Length of 1 in. Total of 1-4, occasionally with a second brood.

FEEDER BEHAVIOR: Does not visit feeders.

COMPARE TO SIMILAR SPECIES: Straight, pointed bill distinguishes from gulls, while size is far smaller than that of most other terns. The Black Tern is the only tern of similar size which shares territory with this species, but possesses conspicuous dark or black coloration throughout the body.

DID YOU KNOW? In the past half-century, Least Tern populations have decreased by 75 to 95%, with contributing factors including the following: domestic cats and dogs predating on their ground-based nests; increased human activity surrounding known breeding colonies; and threats to fish populations due to invasive species, pollutants, and industrial development.

J F M A M J J A S O N D

Adults in breeding plumage at top and bottom (Note: Bill changes in color
to black in Sept., after breeding season has passed).

Adults at top and bottom.

① EASTERN MEADOWLARK. *Sturnella magna.*

SIZE: 9 in.

HABITAT: Somewhat thick fields, grasslands, and prairies.

WILD DIET: Mostly insects, but also seeds and grains (particularly in the winter).

BEHAVIOR: Best known for whistling its distinctive song from elevated perches during breeding season, but is usually less noticeable throughout the remainder of the year, especially in the North. While walking across the ground, forages by probing and prying apart the soil in search of a variety of insects; it accomplishes this feat with its considerably strong jaw muscles. Polygynous by nature, each male will defend a territory of two to three resident females, each with whom he will mate.

MIGRATE? Partially.

NESTING: Selects a small rut in the ground, and constructs nest on top. Cup-shaped, with stems and grasses used. About 8 in. across and 2 in. deep.

EGGS: White to light blue, with brown mottling. Length of 1 in. Total of 3-6, with 2 broods.

BIRD FEEDING TIPS

FEEDER DIET: Cracked corn, hulled sunflower seeds. **FEEDER TYPES**: Ground. **FEEDER BEHAVIOR**: Very uncommon at feeders. Visits are typically during wintertime, when insects are scarce.

COMPARE TO SIMILAR SPECIES: The Western Meadowlark is nearly identical to the Eastern, though their ranges only overlap in the western Midwest U.S. These species are best differentiated by song (Western has flute-like, more garbled two-phrase song, compared to Eastern's higher, clear, one-phrase whistles), though the former is also unreliably identified by the brown lines across its head, which are lighter. Also, this species is somewhat similar to the Dickcissel, but larger size, fully yellow belly, and longer bill are distinct to the meadowlarks.

DID YOU KNOW? While Western Meadowlarks sing about a dozen variations of their common melody, Easterns can have repertoires of over 100 different, but consistent, patterns—each of which still resembles the original song.

J F M A M J J A S O N D

175

⑤ **NORTHERN CARDINAL.** *Cardinalis cardinalis.*

SIZE: 8 ¾ in.

HABITAT: Open woods, cities and suburbs. Also, thickets and scrub.

WILD DIET: Seeds, fruits, and grains. Sometimes, insects.

BEHAVIOR: Conceivably the most photographed bird in North America, this species is often found perched in various shrubs, trees, and even in sheltered surroundings on the ground. Individuals typically stay at each foraging location for several minutes or longer. In late spring and summer, frequently sings from prominent, elevated perches to defend territory. Song is an ascending and whistled *wheet, wheet, ..., wheet,* followed immediately by a quick series of *chew, chew, ..., chew.* Also calls repeatedly with loud metallic chinks.

MIGRATE? No.

NESTING: Prefers locations with dense leaf cover, usually in a tree or shrub. Nest bowl is woven of twigs, and lined with finer grasses, stems. About 3-4 in. across.

EGGS: Off-white to light blue-green, with brown speckling or mottling. Length of 1 in. Total of 2-4, with 2-3 broods.

BIRD FEEDING TIPS

FEEDER DIET: Black-oil and hulled sunflower seeds, safflower seed, peanut hearts, cracked corn, millet, milo. **FEEDER TYPES**: Platforms, hoppers, tubes, ground. **FEEDER BEHAVIOR**: Very common visitor, and one of the first species to repeatedly visit new feeders. Often observed in male-female pairs, especially during spring and summer.

COMPARE TO SIMILAR SPECIES: Male Summer and Scarlet Tanagers are also bright red—particularly the former—but the Northern Cardinal is larger, has a black mask, and has a conspicuous head crest.

DID YOU KNOW? In May and June, cardinals are very territorial toward other individuals of the same species, periodically going so far as to attack their own reflections in windows or panes of glass. Other species—particularly those which nest in the suburbs, such as the American Robin—have also been known to occasionally engage in similar behaviors.

J F M A M J J A S O N D

Adult male at top,
Adult female at bottom left,
Juvenile female at bottom right.

Adults at top and bottom.

④ **GRAY CATBIRD.** *Dumetella carolinensis.*

SIZE: 8 ¾ in.
HABITAT: Thickets, edges of woods, overgrown fields, cities and suburbs.
WILD DIET: Fruits and berries (e.g., holly berries, poison ivy), and insects.
BEHAVIOR: This species is ordinarily sequestered away in tangles of shrubs and vines, hopping about while gleaning fruits and berries from the branches or ground. Most easily recognizable due to its repeated, raspy mewing call—rather like that of a cantankerous feline.
MIGRATE? Partially.
NESTING: Concealed in dense shrub foliage. Bowl of twigs and dried grasses, and lined with softer materials, such as pine needles. About 5-6 in. across.
EGGS: Bright turquoise. Length of 1 in. Total of 1-5, with 2 broods.

BIRD FEEDING TIPS

FEEDER DIET: Mealworms, suet, grape jelly, fruit. **FEEDER TYPES**: Ground, platforms, suet cages. **FEEDER BEHAVIOR**: Uncommon visitor, but known to retrieve suet droppings from ground. Particularly in May and June, may also take mealworms and fruit from platforms.

COMPARE TO SIMILAR SPECIES: Most similar to the larger Northern Mockingbird, but note the Gray Catbird's distinct black head cap, lack of white barring on wings, and overall darker silhouette.

DID YOU KNOW? It is thought that most catbirds which nest along the Atlantic Seaboard winter in Florida or the Caribbean, with most Midwestern birds nesting in Central America. Once the winter is complete, the flocks return to the same local territories where they spent the previous summer—possibly even visiting the same backyards year after year.

J F M A M J J A S O N D

② **EASTERN KINGBIRD.** *Tyrannus tyrannus.*

SIZE: 8 ¼ in.

HABITAT: Fields, edges of woods; often adjacent to lakes, rivers, and wetlands.

WILD DIET: Insects (e.g., dragonflies, crickets). Very occasionally, small fruits.

BEHAVIOR: Often spotted in semi-open country near a water source, perched on the branch of a tree or large bush. It periodically sallies out for insect prey, which is taken both aerially and from swoops near the ground. Individuals usually return to the same perch, even after departures lasting as long as a minute, unless insects are sparse—in which case, a new perch is instead located. Commonly sings with clipped, sputtering notes punctuated by ascending *dzee* notes. Known to flock in groups of several dozen, occasionally larger, during migration periods. As its Latin name suggests, this species is a veritable tyrant in the course of defending its breeding territory from predators and even other kingbirds.

MIGRATE? Yes.

NESTING: Trees and shrubs, at varying heights. Woven cup of dried grasses and twigs, and lined with softer vegetative materials. About 5-6 in. across.

EGGS: Off-white, with large red-brown splotches, usually clustered on oblong side. Length of 1 in. Total of 2-5.

FEEDER BEHAVIOR: Does not visit feeders.

COMPARE TO SIMILAR SPECIES: Much larger than the similarly colored Eastern Phoebe, as well as most other flycatchers.

DID YOU KNOW? The Eastern Kingbird winters in Central and South America, where it breaks with established routine and feeds on an array of small fruits and berries. These wintering sites are mostly concentrated in the western Amazon, and coincide with the wet season—with some localities receiving upwards of 100 inches of rain in just a few months. Fruits quickly begin to burst from their buds all throughout the rainforest—just in time for the famished, travel-wearied kingbird.

J F M A M J J A S O N D

Adults at top and bottom.

Breeding adult at top (Jan. to Aug.),
Nonbreeding adult at bottom left (Sept. to Jan.),
Flock at bottom right (Photo by John Holmes / CC BY-SA / Cropped).

⑤ EUROPEAN STARLING. *Sturnus vulgaris.*

SIZE: 8 ¼ in.

HABITAT: Cities and suburbs, agricultural fields. Often perched on power lines.

WILD DIET: Mostly insects (e.g., grasshoppers, flies) and spiders. Also, fruit and berries, seeds, grains, and garbage.

BEHAVIOR: This invasive species from Europe is most commonly observed in large, wheeling flocks of hundreds, or even thousands, which swarm across the sky—a flocking motion once described by the poet Dante Alighieri as seemingly being pushed by gusts of wind. These birds may forage in agricultural fields, on recently mowed lawns, or in urban centers, exhausting local resources before moving on. Calls include harsh chattering, buzzing, whistling, and rattling noises.

MIGRATE? No.

NESTING: Cavity nester. Selected cavities may include manmade openings (e.g., streetlights), former woodpecker nests, and nest boxes. A shallow bowl is formed inside, constructed of dried grasses. On average, about 8 in. wide.

EGGS: Light blue-green. Length of 1 in. Total of 4-6, with 2 broods.

BIRD FEEDING TIPS

FEEDER DIET: Black-oil and hulled sunflower seeds, suet, cracked corn, peanuts and peanut hearts, millet, oats, milo, fruit. **FEEDER TYPES**: Platforms, hoppers, tubes, ground, suet cages. **FEEDER BEHAVIOR**: Can quickly overrun feeders, a circumstance which can be averted by solely offering safflower seed at some stations. Also, may use nest boxes.

COMPARE TO SIMILAR SPECIES: Very distinctive appearance and profile, and rather unlike most other North American species.

DID YOU KNOW? About 100 starlings were originally introduced to Central Park in 1890 and 1891 by Shakespeare enthusiasts, in homage to a brief account of the species in *Henry IV*. In the years since, however, they have established themselves as one of the most abundant species continent-wide, which has led to the concomitant decline of many native cavity-nesting species, such as the Purple Martin.

J F M A M J J A S O N D

⑤ RED-WINGED BLACKBIRD.
Agelaius phoeniceus.

SIZE: 8 in.

HABITAT: Marshes and ponds, flooded fields, weedy fields. Sometimes along the median strip or roadsides of highways.

WILD DIET: Seeds and grains. In warmer months, half of diet also consists of insects.

BEHAVIOR: The archetypal wetland passerine, or perching bird, this species is known for inhabiting nearby dense tangles of brush and thicket. Opportunistically forages for insects whenever available, and otherwise is a prodigious consumer of seeds and grains. One of the most population-dense species in North America, due to the male's tendency to mate with and defend five to 15 females, and its highly aggressive nest-defense tactics. Song is *kok-a-reeee*, with particular emphasis and length placed on the final, slurred and trilled syllable. This rattling din is just about inescapable in wetter environs.

MIGRATE? Partially.

NESTING: Weaves a neat cup of grasses and reeds, often amid tall shoots of vegetation. About 6 in. across and 4 in. deep.

EGGS: Light turquoise, with dark markings. Length of 1 in. Total of 2-4. Raises 1-3 broods each year, usually 2.

BIRD FEEDING TIPS

FEEDER DIET: Black-oil and hulled sunflower seeds, cracked corn, suet, peanut hearts, oats, millet, milo. **FEEDER TYPES**: Suet cages, platforms, hoppers, tubes. **FEEDER BEHAVIOR**: Most likely to visit in late fall to mid-spring, when insects are less plentiful.

COMPARE TO SIMILAR SPECIES: Male's red-orange wing patch is highly distinctive; female is much smaller and more sparrow-like, but notice her sharp, pointed bill, as well as the defined, light eyeline.

DID YOU KNOW? Males with larger red wing patches are more aggressive and better at defending their territories from rivals. This likely serves as a biological signaling mechanism, and is produced by dietary carotenoid pigments; in fact, this same class of pigments gives carrots their familiar orange hue.

J F M A M J J A S O N D

Adult male at top,
Adult female at bottom left,
Juvenile male at bottom right (Notice "in-between," dirty stage of coloration).

Adult male performing a scratch-and-hop at top,
Adult female at bottom (Photo by Shawn Taylor / CC BY-SA / Cropped).

② EASTERN TOWHEE. *Pipilo erythrophthalmus.*

SIZE: 8 in.

HABITAT: Mostly thickets—in open woods, overgrown fields, and hedgerows.

WILD DIET: Seeds, fruits, buds, insects and spiders, and snails.

BEHAVIOR: This oversized sparrow moves slowly, but noisily, through understories of woods and overgrown fields. Over three-quarters of foraging is conducted on the ground, with occasional forays onto low branches. Prefers to strip away leaf litter to uncover potential food items, often using a characteristic two-legged, backward scratch-and-hop motion. Given the dense cover of its typical habitat, this species is more often seen than heard. Its song resembles *drink-your-teeeeaaaa*, with the final syllable high and trilled; the call is a squeaky, yanking, and ascending *chewink*.

MIGRATE? Mostly.

NESTING: Selects a concealed location on the ground, with the nest sunken into leaf litter amid surrounding vegetation. Finely woven bowl of twigs, grasses, and stems. About 4-5 in. across.

EGGS: Off-white or light pink, with dense, light brown spotting. Length of 1 in. Total of 2-6. Raises 1-3 broods each year, usually 2.

BIRD FEEDING TIPS

FEEDER DIET: Black-oil and hulled sunflower seeds, cracked corn, peanut hearts, millet, milo. **FEEDER TYPES**: Ground, platforms. **FEEDER BEHAVIOR**: Most common in yards with dense shrubbery or hedgerows, particularly near woods with a thicketed understory. Animatedly scratches along the ground for seeds.

COMPARE TO SIMILAR SPECIES: Spotted Towhee of the Great Plains is similar, but has extensive white spotting along the wing. In addition, American Robin also has orange on underside, but Eastern Towhee has a bright white belly.

DID YOU KNOW? The towhee's common name is onomatopoeic, specifically relating to its *towhee* call, which is more often described as a *chewink* (*See* Behavior).

J F M A M J J A S O N D

187

② ROSE-BREASTED GROSBEAK.
Pheucticus ludovicianus.

SIZE: 8 in.

HABITAT: Mostly dense or thicketed woods, also tree-dense parks. During migration, common in suburbs and open woods as well.

WILD DIET: Insects (e.g., beetles, ants), berries (e.g., blackberries, mulberries), seeds, buds, and grains.

BEHAVIOR: Often found in the treetops or amid dense foliage, carefully gleaning any suitable insects or vegetative matter as it hops along. Sings a swooping, up-and-down melody reminiscent of that of the American Robin, but seemingly with more flourishes.

MIGRATE? Yes.

NESTING: Selects a location in the vertical fork of tree branches. Messy cup, woven with twigs. About 7-8 in. across.

EGGS: Off-white to light blue-green, with red-brown spotting. Length of 1 in. Total of 3-4, sometimes with a second brood.

BIRD FEEDING TIPS

FEEDER DIET: Black-oil and hulled sunflower seeds, safflower seed, peanut hearts, cracked corn, oats, millet, milo. **FEEDER TYPES**: Platforms, hoppers, tubes, ground. **FEEDER BEHAVIOR**: Most conspicuous in spring migration, during which large groups are making their way north, and tend to be less fussy regarding habitat selection. Behaves similarly to cardinals, with usual visits of up to a minute and a generally wary disposition.

COMPARE TO SIMILAR SPECIES: Male is highly distinctive. Female may superficially resemble some finches, sparrows, or cowbirds, but has a far stouter bill, pronounced white eyebrow line, and delicate streaking across a pale chest.

DID YOU KNOW? Unlike most birds, the male shares nest incubation responsibilities with the female—often singing happily while doing so.

J F M A M J J A S O N D

Adult male at top (Photo by Johnathan Nightingale / CC BY-SA / Cropped),
Adult female at bottom (Photo by Shawn Taylor / CC BY-SA / Cropped).

Adult female at top (Notice white throat),
Adult male at bottom left (Notice red throat),
Juvenile at bottom right.

MEDIUM BIRDS (6 ½ - 8 ½")

① **YELLOW-BELLIED SAPSUCKER.**
Sphyrapicus varius.

SIZE: 8 in.

HABITAT: Dense to semi-open woods. Often favors woods with plenty of younger, faster-growing trees. Sometimes, orchards.

WILD DIET: Sap, insects (e.g., carpenter ants) and spiders. Sometimes, fruit.

BEHAVIOR: This species drills neat rows of shallow, narrow wells into the inner tissue of tree trunks. These wells are constantly maintained to keep the sap flowing, and further rows are drilled in productive trees to form ordered, dotlike grids. Trees which are frequently used include maples, birches, hickories, and poplars. May also feed on flying insects, and any ants attracted to their sap wells. Idiosyncratic drumming pattern is erratic, and sounds rather like the transmission of an esoteric Morse code message.

MIGRATE? Yes.

NESTING: Excavates a cavity in a dying or decaying tree. Entrance is less than 2 in. across, and nest hole is approximately 9 in. deep.

EGGS: White. Length of 1 in. Total of 4-7.

BIRD FEEDING TIPS

FEEDER DIET: Grape jelly, suet, sugar water, mealworms. **FEEDER TYPES**: Suet cages, platforms, nectar feeders. **FEEDER BEHAVIOR**: Uncommon visitor, but may be regularly attracted by small cups of grape jelly or sugar water, as well as by suet cages.

COMPARE TO SIMILAR SPECIES: Head patterning is particularly distinctive.

DID YOU KNOW? Other species actively benefit from the prolific drilling of sapsuckers, including the porcupines, squirrels, nuthatches, and bats which readily take advantage of the accompanying gratis food source. In addition, hummingbirds have even been known to time spring migrations in line with those of sapsuckers, with breeding success increased by the local presence of open sap wells.

J F M A M J J A S O N D

② PURPLE MARTIN. *Progne subis.*

SIZE: 7 ¾ in.

HABITAT: Cities and suburbs, likely near established martin houses. Often prefers open areas, especially near sources of water.

WILD DIET: Flying insects (e.g., dragonflies, butterflies, grasshoppers, ants).

BEHAVIOR: Circles high in the air, often at heights of 100 to 200 feet, while hunting insects on the wing. Flying motion consists of a quick series of flaps, followed by long, graceful glides. Often found in very large groups, both near established colonies and when roosting in late summer.

MIGRATE? Yes.

NESTING: Colonial cavity nester. Mostly uses martin houses now (*See* Feeder Behavior) due to the omnipresence of invasive European Starlings and House Sparrows, which also use natural cavities. A ragged bowl of twigs is assembled inside the cavity, and is sometimes lined with leaves. About 8 in. across.

EGGS: White. Length of 1 in. Total of 3-6.

FEEDER BEHAVIOR: Does not visit feeders, but does use specially designed martin houses. These elevated birdhouses are painted white and typically consist of multiple compartments, are placed on a pole at a height of 10-18 feet, and are situated in relatively open fields, particularly near water. Some setups also use groupings of gourd-like bulbs. It is crucial to use starling-resistant entrance holes, and to safeguard against ground predators. Individual compartments should be about 8 in. across and 12 in. deep.

COMPARE TO SIMILAR SPECIES: May be confused with similarly sized European Starling, but note the Purple Martin's forked tail, backswept wings, and aerial hawking behavior. Compared to other swallows (which are generally much smaller), male is the only dark-bellied bird, and the female has a dirty, streaked underside.

DID YOU KNOW? Even before the European colonization of the Americas, the Native Americans were known to hang empty gourds for nesting Purple Martins.

J F M A M J J A S O N D

192

Male at top,
Female with male at bottom (Photo by Sam May / CC BY-SA / Cropped).

Adult at top and bottom.

① **WOOD THRUSH.** *Hylocichla mustelina.*

SIZE: 7 ¾ in.

HABITAT: Mature, dense woods. Less commonly, open woods and parks.

WILD DIET: Insects (e.g., beetles, caterpillars, ants), fruit (e.g., elderberries), snails.

BEHAVIOR: This thrush is usually found foraging by itself, sorting through leaf litter with its bill or clambering over low shrubs in search of berries. Individuals are often wary of potential threats, and quickly hop along the forest floor. The Wood Thrush is perhaps best known for its empyrean, bitonal *ee-o-lay* song, which sounds as if it is produced by a duet of skillful flutists. Males usually sing from exposed perches, allowing the melody to drift for acres.

MIGRATE? Yes.

NESTING: Selects a densely vegetated location hidden among the branches of a shrub or low tree. A bowl is woven of twigs and fine grasses, and bound together on the interior with some mud. About 5-6 in. across.

EGGS: Bright turquoise. Length of 1 in. Total of 3-4, with 1-2 broods.

FEEDER BEHAVIOR: Does not visit feeders.

COMPARE TO SIMILAR SPECIES: Similar to other medium-sized thrushes, including the juvenile American Robin, the Veery, the Swainson's Thrush, and the Hermit Thrush. The Wood Thrush is best identified by its red-brown upper side, its white belly with dark, well-defined brown spots, and its brownish, patterned cheek.

DID YOU KNOW? This species has declined significantly over the past number of decades. Nest failures due to the encroachment of Brown-headed Cowbirds is a result of increasing woodland fragmentation, which decreases the amount of deep forest habitat suitable for nesting. Additionally, an academic study coauthored by Miyoko Chu and Stefan Hames of the Cornell Lab of Ornithology has suggested that acid rain may be a supplementary factor, with fewer land snails now available as a calcium source for thrushes when egg-laying.

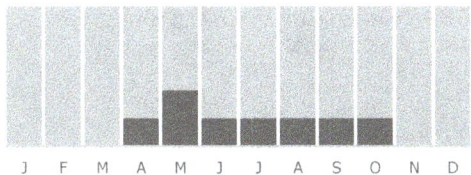

J F M A M J J A S O N D

③ BALTIMORE ORIOLE. *Icterus galbula.*

SIZE: 7 ¾ in.

HABITAT: Open woods, suburbs, parks, and orchards.

WILD DIET: Berries and fruits, insects, and nectar.

BEHAVIOR: Best known for its penchant for gleaning berries and fruits from trees and bushes all across its territory, this species actually takes more insects than fruits during the breeding season—in keeping with the young's higher protein needs. Busily clambers and clings from all angles as it forages for such items as caterpillars, mulberries, and grapes. When feeding on larger fruits, it punctures the surface with its bill, before opening and slurping with deft strokes of its brushlike tongue. In springtime, particularly well-known for its chattering, flute-like whistles.

MIGRATE? Yes.

NESTING: In the upper reaches of a tree, weaves a hanging, bindle-like nest of fine grasses and hairs: a marvel of construction. About 4 in. across and 5 in. deep.

EGGS: Off-white to blue-green, with dark streaking and splotches. Length of 1 in. Total of 3-6.

BIRD FEEDING TIPS

FEEDER DIET: Fruit, grape jelly, sugar water, suet. **FEEDER TYPES**: Platforms, nectar feeders. **FEEDER BEHAVIOR**: Prefers to take orange slices and grape jelly from small platform cups. Also visits nectar feeders. Ceteris paribus, usually attracted to the color orange. More likely to visit feeders outside of breeding season.

COMPARE TO SIMILAR SPECIES: Among males, bright orange underside (compared to smaller Orchard Oriole's dark orange) and full black head and neck are diagnostic. Females have washed-out, yellow-orange coloration on the chest and belly—the only oriole dames with a fully orange-hued underside—and a dirty head and back.

DID YOU KNOW? Despite its fiery plumage, this species is actually a member of the blackbird, or icterid, family.

J F M A M J J A S O N D

Adult male at top,
Adult female at bottom (Note: Juveniles are slightly drabber, buffier by comparison).

Adult male at top,
Adult female at bottom,
Juveniles taking food from adoptive Common Yellowthroat mother, inset.

④ **BROWN-HEADED COWBIRD.** *Molothrus ater.*

SIZE: 7 ½ in.

HABITAT: Edges of woods, open fields, suburbs.

WILD DIET: Seeds, grains, insects. Sometimes eggs of other birds.

BEHAVIOR: Often announces its presence with a short, liquid-like chortle, immediately followed by a thin, high whistle. Customarily forages on the ground, and may also be found perching in trees and bushes. In fields, known to snap up insects disturbed by grazing livestock. Males and females both practice promiscuous mating, with few seasonally established pairs. Juveniles hatch sooner than the young of their host nests (*See* Nesting), and mature much more rapidly; this allows the young cowbird to monopolize resources and frequently outcompete the other members of its cohort.

MIGRATE? Partially.

NESTING: Brood parasite: lays eggs in nests of other birds, usually smaller species (e.g., sparrows, warblers).

EGGS: Off-white, with dense brown speckling. Length of 1 in. Total of 1-4 per nest, with up to 40 eggs per season.

BIRD FEEDING TIPS

FEEDER DIET: Black-oil and hulled sunflower seeds, cracked corn, peanut hearts, suet, millet, oats, milo. **FEEDER TYPES**: Ground, platforms, hoppers, tubes, suet cages. **FEEDER BEHAVIOR**: A highly opportunistic forager, this species is a partisan of feeder setups of nearly all varieties, and may also congregate on the ground for spilled feed. From May to July, juveniles are often observed following adoptive mothers of other species.

COMPARE TO SIMILAR SPECIES: Notice male's distinctive brown head and neck; females and juveniles are duller brown and sparrow-like, but are drabber and lack extensive, well-defined streaking. Also, notice this species' characteristically stout bill, another useful field mark.

DID YOU KNOW? It is thought that the Brown-headed Cowbird's parasitic nesting behavior originally evolved due to necessity, having previously subsisted by following grazing bison across the Great Plains. As it was never in one location for more than a few weeks, it was thus not able to incubate its own young—relying on other species for this task. However, with the fragmentation of woodland due to human development (and the consequent creation of new fringe habitat), this species' further proliferation has seriously threatened populations of many woodland songbirds.

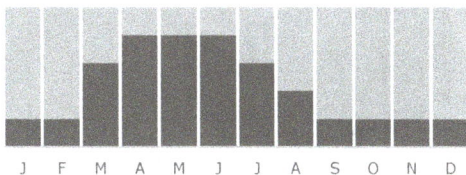

J F M A M J J A S O N D

MEDIUM BIRDS (6 ½ - 8 ½")

① **SPOTTED SANDPIPER.** *Actitis macularius.*

SIZE: 7 ½ in.

HABITAT: Edges of rivers, ponds, and streams. Also, coastlines of oceans, lakes, and reservoirs. Seems to prefer rockier shorelines.

WILD DIET: Mostly insects and insect larvae. Also, small aquatic invertebrates.

BEHAVIOR: Steadily bobs its rear half as it goes about its day, a highly manifest and diagnostic behavior for this species. Often walks in seemingly undeliberate paths near the edge of the water or over rocks—until a quick pecking motion toward prey betrays the earnestness of its original intention. May take insects from the water surface, or even from midair. Usually found by itself or in small groups, though it is likely the most common North American sandpiper, particularly inland.

MIGRATE? Yes.

NESTING: In the vicinity of the water's edge, often tucked away beneath shrubs. May be situated near Common Tern colonies in some locations. A bowl-like scrape is made in the dirt, and lined with leaves and grasses. About 4 in. across.

EGGS: Off-white with brown mottling. Length of 1 - 1 ½ in. Total of 4, sometimes with a second brood.

FEEDER BEHAVIOR: Does not visit feeders.

COMPARE TO SIMILAR SPECIES: Polka-dot pattern on chest during breeding season is very distinctive among shorebirds. In nonbreeding plumage, look for its plain brown back and sides, as well as a white belly and the accompanying white coloration which rises along the sides of its breast.

DID YOU KNOW? Spotted Sandpipers are often polyandrous breeders. In this pattern, females take several mates, laying nests for each individual male to rear. Sequential polyandry of this nature is a rare breeding practice, and limited to just a few shorebird species, of which the Spotted Sandpiper is by far the most common.

J F M A M J J A S O N D

200

Breeding adult at top,
Chick climbing over a stone at bottom left,
Nonbreeding adult at bottom right.

Adults at top and bottom.

① **GREAT CRESTED FLYCATCHER.**
Myiarchus crinitus.

SIZE: 7 ½ in.

HABITAT: Mature, open to semi-open woods; forest clearings.

WILD DIET: Insects (e.g., butterflies, wasps, crickets). Occasionally, small fruits.

BEHAVIOR: Perches and flies high amid the treetops, exploiting a relatively unique ecological niche among the flycatchers. Individuals sally out for insect prey for longer periods of time, and are resultantly much less likely than other flycatchers to return to the same perch. Like many flycatchers, can be entertaining to watch in flight, as it darts and swoops in close pursuit of its prey. Sometimes observed nodding its head while perched, and singing with a variety of buzzing, ascending, *breep*-like whistles.

MIGRATE? Yes.

NESTING: Cavity nester. May use natural tree hollows, former woodpecker nests, and nesting boxes. Prefers hole with a depth of 5-8 in. Inside, constructs a loosely hewn bowl of grasses, twigs, and various debris. Bowl is about 3 in. across.

EGGS: Off-white to pink, with extensive dark red-brown splotching. Length of ¾ in. Total of 4-7.

FEEDER BEHAVIOR: Does not visit feeders, but does use nest boxes.

COMPARE TO SIMILAR SPECIES: Yellow belly, conspicuous crest, and rufous tail distinguish from other flycatchers.

DID YOU KNOW? This species is known to weave molted snakeskins into its nests whenever possible, particularly in regions where there are more prolific snake populations, such as in Georgia, Louisiana, and Florida. Some titmice also practice this behavior, which may attempt to discourage ovivorous (or egg-eating) trespassers from frequenting the nest.

J F M A M J J A S O N D

203

MEDIUM BIRDS (6 ½ - 8 ½")

③ **EASTERN BLUEBIRD.** *Sialia sialis.*

SIZE: 7 ¼ in.

HABITAT: Open country with some trees, including the following locations: rural fields, parks, golf courses, roadsides, orchards, open woods, and suburbs.

WILD DIET: Insects (e.g., grasshoppers, crickets), fruit and berries.

BEHAVIOR: Bluebirds are often found on lone or exposed perches (e.g., power lines, sign posts, tree branches), scanning the ground for insects. Once a movement has been recognized, the individual swoops to the ground, quickly takes the insect, and returns to a perch. Bluebirds may also glean fruits and berries in fall and winter, when insects are far less plentiful. A mildly varied repertoire of songs and calls includes sweet, warbling whistles and quick, raspy chattering.

MIGRATE? Partially.

NESTING: Cavity nester. Uses natural tree hollows, former woodpecker nests, and nest boxes. A plain, cramped bowl of dried grasses is woven and pressed together. Cavity is about 4-6 in. wide, with an entrance under 2 in. in diameter.

EGGS: Light blue-green. Length of ¾ in. Total of 3-7. Usually raises 2 broods each year, sometimes attempting to hatch and raise a third.

BIRD FEEDING TIPS

FEEDER DIET: Mealworms, fruit, suet, peanut hearts, black-oil and hulled sunflower seeds.
FEEDER TYPES: Platforms, tubes, ground. **FEEDER BEHAVIOR**: May gather in small flocks, particularly if live mealworms are offered. Visits yards with native berry bushes in colder months. Also, uses manmade nest boxes (*See* Nesting).

COMPARE TO SIMILAR SPECIES: Somewhat similar to the Mountain Bluebird of the Rockies, but Eastern is the only resident bluebird with an orange wash on its breast. The smaller Tufted Titmouse has a conspicuous head crest, and a greyish back and tail.

DID YOU KNOW? The Eastern Bluebird's vision is well suited to its perch-and-pursuit hunting strategy, with individuals able to spot insects from over 25 yards.

J F M A M J J A S O N D

204

Male at top,
Female at bottom left,
Juvenile at bottom right.

Adults at top and bottom left,
Silhouette in flight at bottom right.

④ **BARN SWALLOW.** *Hirundo rustica.*

SIZE: 7 in.

HABITAT: Various open fields (both suburban and rural), and over wetlands and lakes.

WILD DIET: Flying insects (e.g., flies, butterflies, aphids).

BEHAVIOR: Flies somewhat low over open country or water, snapping up large flying insects with its cavernous mouth. Wingbeats are quick, agile, and moderately shallow. Flocks are known to follow large machinery or livestock to feed on the insects disturbed by the activity. When flying over water, frequently dips to the surface, drinking and bathing while on the wing. Cheerfully jabbers while flying, often making *cheep* or *chureep* calls.

MIGRATE? Yes.

NESTING: Previously nested in caves, but now nests almost exclusively in barns and similar, artificial structures. Nest is a mud-and-grass mixture; this dries into a relatively firm cup, which is affixed to a vertical wall or horizontal beam. May be reused in future years. About 5-8 in. across.

EGGS: Off-white or light pink, with dark brown spotting. Length of ¾ in. Total of 3-6, with 1-2 broods.

FEEDER BEHAVIOR: Does not visit feeders.

COMPARE TO SIMILAR SPECIES: Orange underside and long, forked tail are very different than those of most other swallows. Cliff and Cave Swallows may have some orange on underside, but are much smaller and lack a strongly forked tail.

DID YOU KNOW? Unmated males sometimes enter the nests of established breeding pairs, killing all of the nestlings. This allows the encroacher to then breed with the previously mated female, often producing a second, viable brood.

J F M A M J J A S O N D

① **VEERY.** *Catharus fuscescens.*

SIZE: 7 in.

HABITAT: Semi-dense woods, usually near a stream, wetland, or river. Sometimes prefers a thicketed understory.

WILD DIET: Insects (e.g., beetles, caterpillars), fruit (e.g., blueberries).

BEHAVIOR: Furtively probes through leaf litter with use of its bill, hopping along as it searches for insects and berries—the latter of which may also be obtained by directly gleaning from a branch. Occasionally takes flying insects out of the air with brief, deliberate flights. So named for its *veer* calls, which are down-slurred, metallic, and sometimes burbling.

MIGRATE? Yes.

NESTING: Selects a concealed location on or near the ground, amid brushy vegetation. Cup-shaped nest is constructed with leaves, bark, twigs, stems, and other plant fibers. About 6 in. across.

EGGS: Bright turquoise. Length of 1 in. Total of 3-4, sometimes with a second brood.

FEEDER BEHAVIOR: Does not visit feeders.

COMPARE TO SIMILAR SPECIES: Similar to other medium-sized thrushes, including the juvenile American Robin, the Wood Thrush, the Swainson's Thrush, and the Hermit Thrush (particularly the last two). The Veery has the least-spotted underside of those mentioned, with very light, almost indistinct tawny spotting on the upper breast. It also lacks a bold, white eye-ring like that of the Swainson's or Hermit.

DID YOU KNOW? Like many birds, the Veery varies its diet seasonally. During the breeding season, when more protein is often needed, this species primarily feeds on insects. Before and during migration, it instead consumes vast quantities of fruits and berries, providing an optimal energy source for long evening flights.

J F M A M J J A S O N D

Adult at top,
Adult at bottom (Photo by Andy Reago, Chrissy McClarren / CC BY-SA / Cropped).

Breeding adult at top (Note: This individual's legs have been banded for research puposes),
Nonbreeding adult at bottom.

② SEMIPALMATED PLOVER.
Charadrius semipalmatus.

SIZE: 7 in.

HABITAT: Mostly beaches and mudflats. During migration, this may include locations along a variety of smaller lakes, reservoirs, and even flooded fields; however, wintering sites are more strictly limited to oceanic coastlines.

WILD DIET: Worms, aquatic invertebrates, and insects.

BEHAVIOR: This shorebird species is often observed in loose flocks, foraging along intertidal zones or mudflats for stranded worms and invertebrates. Individuals frenetically run, pause, and repeat as they scan for potential prey items—seldom wading into water more than an inch deep. The plovers peck in the direction of any movement in the substrate, with keen eyesight enabling the detection of worms and invertebrates up to a few inches below the surface. Call is a squeaky, rising *chweep*, which may also be uttered while foraging.

MIGRATE? Yes.

NESTING: Breeds along the tundral wetlands of northern Canada and Alaska. A very shallow nest scrape is made in the gravel, and lined with twigs and other vegetative debris. About 3 in. across.

EGGS: Off-white, with large dark spotting. Length of 1 ½ in. Total of 4.

FEEDER BEHAVIOR: Does not visit feeders.

COMPARE TO SIMILAR SPECIES: Similar to the much larger Killdeer, but has brighter orange legs, and only features one dark breast band (rather than two).

DID YOU KNOW? The Semipalmated Plover is named for the partial webbing present between its toes. This allows the plover to swim across narrow channels of water while foraging, though it seems to rarely employ this faculty—instead, normally taking short flights between feeding or roosting areas.

J F M A M J J A S O N D

211

② SCARLET TANAGER. *Piranga olivacea.*

SIZE: 7 in.

HABITAT: Dense, mature woods. During migration, also common in open woods, parks, and suburbs.

WILD DIET: Insects (e.g., ants, dragonflies, wasps) and spiders, sometimes fruit.

BEHAVIOR: This species of the treetops uses a variety of methods to capture its invertebrate prey. While foraging, Scarlet Tanagers have been known to walk along horizontal branches, vertically cling to bark, hover near flocks of flying insects, or even sally out with short, direct flights like a flycatcher. Up-and-down song is like that of an American Robin, but noticeably hoarser.

MIGRATE? Yes.

NESTING: Selects a high, sheltered location in the outer branches of a tree. Thick, sloppily constructed bowl of twigs and grasses. About 5 in. across.

EGGS: Pale blue-green, with light brown mottling. Length of 1 in. Total of 4.

BIRD FEEDING TIPS

FEEDER DIET: Fruit, grape jelly, mealworms, suet. **FEEDER TYPES**: Platforms. **FEEDER BEHAVIOR**: Uncommon, and normally only visits feeders during migration—particularly if there are insufficient numbers of insects (perhaps owing to a late spring).

COMPARE TO SIMILAR SPECIES: Most similar to the related Summer Tanager; males differ by way of their jet-black wings and tail, while females tend to be a much greener shade of yellow. Bright red coloration of males might also suggest a Northern Cardinal, though this cardinalid has a distinctive head crest and a frequently more upright posture.

DID YOU KNOW? This species has begun to experience increased nest failures near clearings and edges of woods, particularly due to the spread of the Brown-headed Cowbird, a fringe habitat specialist. This has contributed to the recent decline of tanager populations—an issue facing other regional songbirds as well.

Breeding male at top,
Nonbreeding male at bottom left (in Sept. or Oct.),
Female at bottom right (Photo by Félix Uribe / CC BY-SA / Cropped).

Adult males at top and bottom left,
Adult females at bottom right.

① **BOBOLINK.** *Dolichonyx oryzivorus.*

SIZE: 7 in.

HABITAT: Overgrown fields and grasslands. Sometimes near wetlands.

WILD DIET: Seeds, insects and insect larvae, spiders, grains.

BEHAVIOR: A bird of meadows and prairies, this species is often found perched atop grassy stems, gleaning seeds from within the plant fibers. It also forages on the ground from time to time, particularly when taking insects and spiders. Both sexes are promiscuous with mating, and males are quite active when defending their territories, chasing rivals back and forth among the grasses. Emits a complex, liquid-like, and effervescent song, especially when in flight.

MIGRATE? Yes.

NESTING: Scrapes a depression in the ground amid a cover of dense vegetation. Finely woven bowl of dried grasses and stems. About 4 in. across.

EGGS: Light blue to rufous, with rusty mottling. Length of ¾ in. Total of 4-6.

FEEDER BEHAVIOR: Does not visit feeders.

COMPARE TO SIMILAR SPECIES: Males are very distinctive, especially in typical habitat. Females are plainer in color and thus may bear a passing resemblance to some grassland sparrows, but note that the female Bobolink is much larger and features a pale, beige underside.

DID YOU KNOW? Bobolinks are prodigious migrators, flying over 12,000 miles between northern North America and central South America twice yearly. Like many birds, this species is able to navigate by use of the Earth's magnetic field; in this case, magnetized iron oxides are present inside each bird's skull, closely bordering the olfactory nerves. This means that, loosely speaking, Bobolinks are able to actively *smell* their heading with specific reference to magnetic north and south.

J F M A M J J A S O N D

215

MEDIUM BIRDS (6 ½ - 8 ½")

② **FOX SPARROW.** *Passerella iliaca.*

SIZE: 6 ¾ in.
HABITAT: Thicketed woods, brush, suburbs.
WILD DIET: Seeds, fruits, buds, insects and spiders.
BEHAVIOR: One of the first migrants to move north in the spring—and one of the last to return south in the fall—this plump, attractive sparrow prefers to inhabit brushy, obscured spots in the thicketed understory of woods. Like many larger sparrows and towhees, the Fox Sparrow tends to scratch-and-hop with both legs to uncover hidden tidbits from beneath debris. Song is an abbreviated melody of short chips and whistles.
MIGRATE? Yes.
NESTING: In the East, breeds mostly in Canada. Situated low in shrubs or evergreens, nest is a messy, thick cup of twigs and grasses. About 5-8 in. wide.
EGGS: Light blue-green, with thick brown mottling. Length of ¾ in. Total of 3-5.

BIRD FEEDING TIPS

FEEDER DIET: Black-oil and hulled sunflower seeds, cracked corn, millet, milo, nyjer. **FEEDER TYPES**: Ground, platforms. **FEEDER BEHAVIOR**: Known to conspicuously scrape-hop the ground with both legs to uncover fallen seeds. Not usually found together in large numbers, but may loosely associate with flocks of other sparrow species.

COMPARE TO SIMILAR SPECIES: Similar to Song Sparrow, but much larger with reddish-brown coloring. May also be confused with the similarly sized Hermit Thrush, but note the stouter, shorter bill and chunkier overall silhouette of the Fox Sparrow.

DID YOU KNOW? There are four distinct subspecies of the Fox Sparrow, each with separate geographies, differing physical characteristics, and distinct songs. These include the Red Fox Sparrow of central and eastern North America (pictured in all examples at left), the Sooty of the Pacific Coast, and the Slate-colored and Thick-billed of the interior West.

J F M A M J J A S O N D

Adult at top (Photo by Dominic Sherony / CC BY-SA / Cropped),
Adult at bottom (Photo by Kim Taylor Hull / CC BY-SA).

Adults at top and bottom.

④ **WHITE-THROATED SPARROW.**
Zonotrichia albicollis.

SIZE: 6 ¾ in.

HABITAT: Thicketed woods, hedgerows, suburbs.

WILD DIET: Seeds (e.g., of grasses), fruits and berries, insects and spiders.

BEHAVIOR: Forages by hopping along the ground as it combs through leaf litter and vegetative debris. This species rummages for food by quickly scraping both feet along the ground, or by nudging away smaller items with the bill. May form somewhat large, loose flocks in some wintering territories. Song is a very distinctive, high-whistled *Oh-Can-a-da*, with the final three tones delivered at the same, higher pitch.

MIGRATE? Yes.

NESTING: Usually placed on the ground, sheltered beneath shrubs. Bowl is woven with fine grasses and stems. About 4 in. across.

EGGS: Off-white to light blue-green, with light brown splotching. Length of ¾ in. Total of 3-6, occasionally with a second brood.

BIRD FEEDING TIPS

FEEDER DIET: Black-oil and hulled sunflower seeds, cracked corn, millet, milo. **FEEDER TYPES**: Ground, platforms. **FEEDER BEHAVIOR**: Relatively common visitor. Most often found on the ground as it forages for fallen seeds. May sometimes be outcompeted by other species of sparrows.

COMPARE TO SIMILAR SPECIES: Most similar to the White-crowned Sparrow, its close relative. Key differences include the White-throated's yellow spot in front of the eyes, as well as its namesake, bold-white throat.

DID YOU KNOW? On rare occasions, this species may nest aboveground in the branches of trees—but only if a first nest attempt has failed, normally due to predation. Common nest predators include grackles, jays, squirrels, and outdoor housecats.

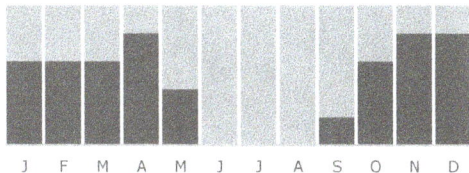

J F M A M J J A S O N D

219

③ CEDAR WAXWING. *Bombycilla cedrorum.*

SIZE: 6 ½ in.

HABITAT: Open woods, orchards, overgrown fields, and suburbs.

WILD DIET: Primarily fruit and berries. Also, some insects during breeding season.

BEHAVIOR: This frugivorous species is most often found wherever wild fruits and berries are available. Forages for berries by hovering or stooping down from a branch; when pursuing insects, makes darting, agile flights from exposed perches. Congregates in medium to large-sized flocks, though some birds may wander a few hundred feet away near the fringes. Calls are repeated, high-pitched *tsee* notes.

MIGRATE? Partially.

NESTING: In a fork of tree branches, constructs a bowl of variable depth using woven twigs and grasses. About 5 in. across.

EGGS: Shades of blue-green, with dark spots. Length of ¾ in. Total of 4-7, occasionally with a second brood.

BIRD FEEDING TIPS

FEEDER DIET: Fruit. **FEEDER TYPES**: Platforms. **FEEDER BEHAVIOR**: Extremely uncommon at feeders, but likely to repeatedly visit yards with extensive plantings of native berry bushes and trees. However, do *not* plant the ornamental shrub *Nandina domestica*, also known as heavenly bamboo, as its berries are highly toxic to waxwings and other frugivorous (i.e., fruit-eating) birds.

COMPARE TO SIMILAR SPECIES: Closely resembles the Bohemian Waxwing, which is native to the evergreen forests of southern and central Canada, and may wander south in winters if there is an insufficient food supply. The Bohemian is much stouter, and has a grayish (rather than yellow) belly.

DID YOU KNOW? Waxwings are well-known for their habit of inadvertently consuming large quantities of overripe—and, therefore, fermenting—berries, a behavior which causes acute onset drunkenness. As a result, individuals may stagger about, fly repeatedly into cars and windows, and generally create a considerable hullabaloo.

J F M A M J J A S O N D

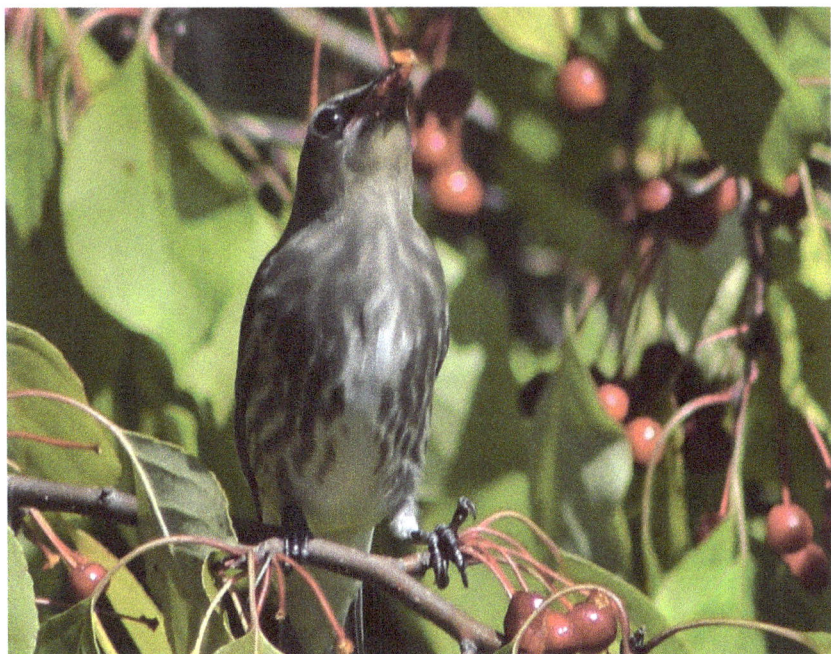

Adult at top,
Juvenile at bottom.

Adult at top,
Juvenile at bottom.

① WHITE-CROWNED SPARROW.
Zonotrichia leucophrys.

SIZE: 6 ½ in.

HABITAT: Thickets, overgrown fields, and suburbs.

WILD DIET: Seeds (e.g., of grasses), insects and spiders, berries, and grains.

BEHAVIOR: More active than some other sparrows, this handsome species hurriedly forages on the ground—moving by hopping, and displacing leaf litter by scratching the ground with both feet. Individuals are typically perched in brushy vegetation or on the ground, irregularly darting in and out of cover. This species' song is a cheerful mix of whistles, metallic rings, and trills, which varies regionally.

MIGRATE? No.

NESTING: Selects a concealed location amid the tangles of a shrub. Bowl of twigs, grasses, and stems with a messy outer rim. About 5 in. across.

EGGS: Shades of blue-green, with light brown mottling. Length of ¾ in. Total of 3-6, with 2-3 broods.

BIRD FEEDING TIPS

FEEDER DIET: Black-oil and hulled sunflower seeds, cracked corn, millet, milo. **FEEDER TYPES**: Ground, platforms. **FEEDER BEHAVIOR**: Ordinarily found on the ground, gleaning fallen seeds. May be accompanied by other species of sparrows.

COMPARE TO SIMILAR SPECIES: Most similar to the White-throated Sparrow, its close relative. Key differences include the White-throated's yellow spot in front of the eyes, as well as its namesake, bold white throat.

DID YOU KNOW? A group of field naturalists led by Elizabeth Derryberry found that this species' songs substantively increased in both clarity and overall range of pitch during the recent COVID-19 pandemic. This study took place in San Francisco, CA, with the cause thought to be reduced traffic noise.

J F M A M J J A S O N D

② **ORCHARD ORIOLE.** *Icterus spurius.*

SIZE: 6 ½ in.

HABITAT: Open woods, thickets, and orchards. Particularly, habitats which also feature a nearby water edge (e.g., river or stream, lake, wetland).

WILD DIET: Mostly insects; also, fruits and nectar.

BEHAVIOR: Often found in the treetops, scrambling about as it gleans insects from the branches and leaves. Immediately before spring and fall migrations, this species dramatically ramps up its fruit and nectar intake; the sugars found in these foods are more easily converted to fuel for the long migration ahead.

MIGRATE? Yes.

NESTING: Hangs a distinctive, bag-like nest from an outer tree branch. Woven with fine grasses and fibers. About 4 in. across and 3 in. deep.

EGGS: Off-white to light blue, with brown splotches. Length of ¾ in. Total of 4-7.

BIRD FEEDING TIPS

FEEDER DIET: Fruit, grape jelly, sugar water. **FEEDER TYPES**: Platforms, nectar feeders. **FEEDER BEHAVIOR**: Less common feeder visitor than Baltimore Oriole; most observed at feeders outside of breeding season and during times of relative insect scarcity. Entertaining to watch, particularly as it drinks from orange slices—a staple for orioles of all stripes.

COMPARE TO SIMILAR SPECIES: Smaller than the Baltimore Oriole; males have a deeper, currant-red underside, while females and juveniles feature a light yellow.

DID YOU KNOW? Like many hummingbirds, the Orchard Oriole is particularly fond of the nectar of the trumpet creeper. It is known for perching near each flower and reaching inside with its bill, providing a valuable cross-pollination service in the process. However, it is not averse to simply piercing the flowers at the base to access the nectar: a more direct technique that is decidedly less beneficial for the plant.

J F M A M J J A S O N D

Adult male at top (Photo by Becky Matsubara / CC BY-SA / Cropped),
Adult female at bottom (Photo by Andrew Weitzel / CC BY-SA / Cropped).

Adult male at top (Notice red on back of head),
Adult female at bottom.

⑤ DOWNY WOODPECKER. *Dryobates pubescens.*

SIZE: 6 ¼ in.

HABITAT: Open woods, suburbs.

WILD DIET: Mostly insects. Also, nuts (e.g., acorns), seeds, and berries.

BEHAVIOR: The smallest of the North American woodpeckers, this sparrow-sized bird is most often found industriously pecking away at tree bark. The beetles, ants, and larvae which are most often gleaned during this process constitute the majority of its diet, though this species is an exceedingly common backyard feeder visitor (particularly in winter). Commonly gives a high, squeaky *pic* call, and forms flocks much more readily than most other woodpecker species.

MIGRATE? No.

NESTING: Excavates a small cavity beneath a knob, often in a decaying tree. About 1 - 1 ½ in. across and 9 in. deep.

EGGS: White. Length of ¾ in. Total of 4-6, occasionally with a second brood.

BIRD FEEDING TIPS

FEEDER DIET: Suet, black-oil and hulled sunflower seeds, peanuts and peanut hearts, mealworms, safflower seed. **FEEDER TYPES**: Suet cages, hoppers, platforms, tubes. **FEEDER BEHAVIOR**: Acrobatically clings to hoppers or tubes, or pecks at suet cages. May arrive in small flocks if sufficient food sources available. During the breeding season, may be observed entertainingly chasing its conspecifics around and among the trees.

COMPARE TO SIMILAR SPECIES: Most similar to the larger Hairy Woodpecker, which is taller than the height of a standard suet cage. Downy has a bill shorter than the length of its head, and black spotting on its outer white tail feathers.

DID YOU KNOW? The Downy is a well-known predator of larvae of the invasive European corn borer, a moth which causes over $1 billion in yearly damages to the North American agricultural industry. This moth lays its eggs on the ears of corn, and larvae burrow into the crop as they rapidly mature and metamorphose.

J F M A M J J A S O N D

⑤ HOUSE SPARROW. *Passer domesticus.*

SIZE: 6 ¼ in.

HABITAT: Cities, suburbs, farms.

WILD DIET: Seeds, grains, garbage, insects and spiders.

BEHAVIOR: If sparrows are present on a sidewalk or flowerbed in any variety of urban environment, they are almost always members of this invasive species. House Sparrows tend to form large, noisy flocks, which feature surprisingly rigid hierarchical structures: older males have more black on the breast and throat, while younger individuals may tremulously flick their tails when approached by elders. Between foraging sessions, several dozen individuals may perch in nearby trees or bushes. Vocalizations are a mix of *chrip* and *churrip* notes.

MIGRATE? No.

NESTING: Often colonial. Uses natural and manmade cavities, such as tree hollows, eaves of houses, and dilapidated roofs. A tight cup of grasses and stems is lined with feathers, and may be adjacent to another nest. About 5 in. wide.

EGGS: Off-white to light blue-green, with brown speckling. Length of ¾ in. Total of 4-6. Raises 2-4 broods each year, usually 3.

BIRD FEEDING TIPS

FEEDER DIET: Black-oil and hulled sunflower seeds, millet, peanut hearts, cracked corn, milo, suet. **FEEDER TYPES**: Ground, platforms, hoppers, tubes. **FEEDER BEHAVIOR**: Often present in large, semi-localized flocks, which may overrun feeders. May claim, and even evict existing tenants of, nest boxes.

COMPARE TO SIMILAR SPECIES: Compared to New World sparrows and finches, the black throat and breast of male are distinctive. Generally, its habitat and chunky profile are the clearest giveaways, along with the presence of nearby, identifiable males.

DID YOU KNOW? House Sparrows, even if fully or partially blinded, are able to maintain a consistent circadian rhythm, owing to photoreceptors located inside the skull.

J F M A M J J A S O N D

Adult male at top,
Adult female at bottom.

Adult male at top (Photo by Andrew Weitzel / CC BY-SA / Cropped),
Adult female at bottom (Photo by Katja Schulz / CC BY-SA).

① **BLUE GROSBEAK.** *Passerina caerulea.*

SIZE: 6 ¼ in.

HABITAT: Thickets, open woods, and scrub. Sometimes, agricultural fields.

WILD DIET: Insects (e.g., crickets) and spiders, snails, seeds, grains, and fruit.

BEHAVIOR: Warbles and chinks amid dense tangles of vines and saplings, making this bird elusive in the field—and particularly difficult to clearly photograph. Usually forages by hopping on the ground, snatching small invertebrates and fallen plant matter from pockets in the brush. From late spring through summer, males sing from exposed perches while defending individual territories of up to 25 acres, leading to lower relative population densities. Most likely to flock during migration.

MIGRATE? Yes.

NESTING: Selects a secluded location less than 10 ft. above the ground, in branches of trees or shrubs. Neatly woven cup of twigs and stems. About 3-4 in. across.

EGGS: Off-white to light blue-green. Length of ¾ in. Total of 3-5, with 2 broods.

BIRD FEEDING TIPS

FEEDER DIET: Black-oil and hulled sunflower seeds, cracked corn, millet, oats, milo.
FEEDER TYPES: Ground, platforms. **FEEDER BEHAVIOR**: Most likely to visit feeders in late summer or early fall—just before migration—as it tops off energy stores for the long flights ahead.

COMPARE TO SIMILAR SPECIES: Male and female resemble their Indigo Bunting counterparts, but note the following: Blue Grosbeaks are larger with a much more sizable bill, and the male is a deeper blue (i.e., indigo, rather than cerulean).

DID YOU KNOW? A flock of grosbeaks is known as a "gross." This also applies to other grosbeak species, such as the Pine and Rose-breasted varieties.

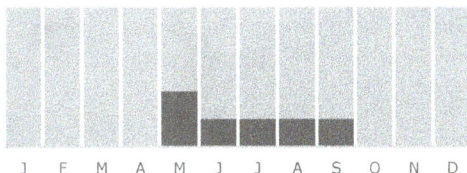

J F M A M J J A S O N D

③ **EASTERN PHOEBE.** *Sayornis phoebe.*

SIZE: 6 in.

HABITAT: Suburbs, open woods, field edges. Sometimes near sources of water.

WILD DIET: Flying insects. In colder months, may eat small fruits or berries.

BEHAVIOR: This dusky, solitary bird may initially seem inconspicuous for passive observers; however, it is among the first migrants to arrive in the spring, and perches on open branches while mirthfully bobbing its tail up and down. After frequent, darting flights out for prey, it almost always returns to the same perch, though it may select a new perch if insects are no longer present nearby. Its penchant for inhabiting open areas near houses, particularly during spring and fall migration, means that suburbanites will quickly grow familiar with this species' raspy, whistled *fee-bree*—repeated in tidy couplets all throughout the day.

MIGRATE? Yes.

NESTING: Prefers a rocky nook or cranny, often under manmade overhangs (e.g., eaves of roofs, fissures in concrete, etc.). Bowl of dried grasses and vegetation. About 6 in. across.

EGGS: Off-white to light pink, with mild speckling. Length of ¾ in. Total of 3-5, with 2 broods.

FEEDER BEHAVIOR: Does not normally visit feeders, though there have been rare reports of this species taking dried mealworms when food is scarce. May use nest boxes.

COMPARE TO SIMILAR SPECIES: The Eastern Wood-Pewee is of similar size and coloration. In particular, note the Eastern Phoebe's more slumped posture, darker head cap, and short, black bill.

DID YOU KNOW? Eastern Phoebes have successfully adapted their nesting habits to the ever-increasing presence of humankind, having previously used sheltered, rocky ledges. Some phoebes have even been observed nesting in the spaces vacated by fallen bricks in below-ground wells.

J F M A M J J A S O N D

Adult at top,
Juvenile at bottom (Notice light yellow on belly).

Adult male at top,
Adult female at bottom.

⑤ DARK-EYED JUNCO. *Junco hyemalis.*

SIZE: 6 in.

HABITAT: Open to semi-open woods, thickets, parks, and suburbs.

WILD DIET: Mostly seeds, also insects and spiders.

BEHAVIOR: This species is most often associated with its flocking behavior during the winter months, when hosts of up to several dozen drip from the trees and populate clearings on the ground—all the while singing with soft, sweet, whistled trills. At foraging sites with ample resources, other species of sparrows may associate with juncos, forming busy, mixed flocks. Females tend to winter farther south than many males, as they are socially subordinate given their slightly smaller size. Like many small, flocking birds, this species tends to be a prime target for Cooper's and Sharp-shinned Hawks, which may monitor suburban feeders with particularly well-established avian denizens.

MIGRATE? Yes.

NESTING: Selects a concealed, brushy depression in the ground. Cup-shaped nest is finely woven of grasses. About 5 in. across.

EGGS: Off white to light blue, with various brown markings. Length of ¾ in. Total of 3-5, with 2 broods.

BIRD FEEDING TIPS

FEEDER DIET: Millet, milo, black-oil and hulled sunflower seeds, nyjer, peanut hearts, cracked corn, safflower seed, suet. **FEEDER TYPES**: Ground, platforms. **FEEDER BEHAVIOR**: Gathers in rather large, peaceable flocks. When arriving, tends to aerially dart from a nearby tree or shrub, descending to the ground beneath the feeders.

COMPARE TO SIMILAR SPECIES: Very much a *sui generis*, two-toned sparrow.

DID YOU KNOW? There are six separate North American subspecies of junco, each of which was formerly classified as its own species. The Slate-colored taxon is pictured at left, and is the only common variety in this region. However, the brown-sided Oregon Junco may arrive as a vagrant from its typical westerly range, and is known to flock with Slate-coloreds in such cases.

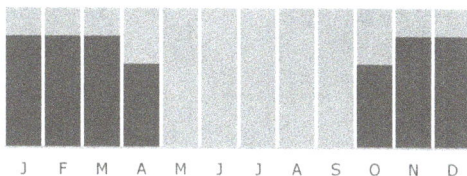

J F M A M J J A S O N D

② AMERICAN TREE SPARROW.
Spizelloides arborea.

SIZE: 6 in.

HABITAT: Overgrown fields, edges of wetlands, open woods, and suburbs.

WILD DIET: Seeds (e.g., of grasses), berries, insects and spiders.

BEHAVIOR: The American Tree Sparrow's name is a certifiable misnomer, with individuals ordinarily found foraging near the ground in weedy or brushy areas. This species hops along as it busily gleans fallen seeds and low-hanging berries, with insects and spiders only a significant part of the diet during the summer months. When foraging, may emit brief, chattering calls.

MIGRATE? Yes.

NESTING: Breeds in northern Canada and Alaska, in tundra scrub. Nest is a grassy cup on the ground, partly hidden by surrounding vegetation and lined with grouse feathers. About 4-5 in. across.

EGGS: Shades of blue-green, with brown speckling. Length of ¾ in. Total of 4-6.

BIRD FEEDING TIPS

FEEDER DIET: Millet, black-oil and hulled sunflower seeds, nyjer, milo, peanut hearts, cracked corn. **FEEDER TYPES**: Ground, platforms, hoppers, tubes. **FEEDER BEHAVIOR**: Semi-frequent visitor during the cold winter months, usually in small groups.

COMPARE TO SIMILAR SPECIES: Similar to Field and Chipping Sparrows, but noticeably larger and plumper than both. Also, notice its characteristic, dark breast spot and bicolored bill.

DID YOU KNOW? A group of sparrows is frequently called a host, crew, or meinie (e.g., a host of sparrows).

J F M A M J J A S O N D

Adults at top and bottom.

Breeding adult at top,
Nonbreeding adult at bottom.

② SEMIPALMATED SANDPIPER. *Calidris pusilla.*

SIZE: 6 in.

HABITAT: Coastal beaches, mudflats, and wetlands.

WILD DIET: Insects (e.g., midges) and spiders, aquatic invertebrates and worms.

BEHAVIOR: This small sandpiper is most often observed on mudflats or in very shallow water, where it conducts the majority of its foraging activities. Individuals haltingly walk along while probing or jabbing into the water or substrate; when in large, loose flocks during migratory periods, individuals also noisily squabble as they fight over prime feeding areas. While normally most active by day, this sandpiper may also feed at dark with the aid of its adaptively dilating pupils and sensitive bill—particularly when gaining weight for upcoming migration flights.

MIGRATE? Yes.

NESTING: Breeds in the tundra of northern Canada and Alaska. Selects a grassy or mossy patch, often near wetlands and along a slight rise. A shallow nest scrape is made in the soil, and lined with plant materials. About 2-3 in. across.

EGGS: Off-white, with large dark spotting. Length of 1 in. Total of 4.

FEEDER BEHAVIOR: Does not visit feeders.

COMPARE TO SIMILAR SPECIES: Most similar to the less common Western Sandpiper. During breeding season, the Semipalmated lacks the Western's bold, orange tinges across the sides of its head and folded wings. In fall and winter, both species become mostly grey, with white undersides; however, the Semipalmated has a darker head cap at this time. Additionally, the similar Least Sandpiper has distinctive yellow legs, unlike the dark legs of the Semipalmated.

DID YOU KNOW? The Semipalmated Sandpiper is a member of the *peeps*, a group of small sandpipers which includes the Semipalmated, Least, and Western Sandpipers. The larger White-rumped, Baird's, and Pectoral Sandpipers are also sometimes included, as they are fellow members of the *Calidris* genus.

J F M A M J J A S O N D

239

④ **TUFTED TITMOUSE.** *Baeolophus bicolor.*

SIZE: 6 in.

HABITAT: Dense woods, wooded parks, and suburbs.

WILD DIET: Insects (e.g., caterpillars, wasps) and spiders, nuts (e.g., acorns), seeds, berries.

BEHAVIOR: A lively, nimble bird of the forests, this species restlessly flits from branch to branch: only taking fitful spells of rest when plotting its next foraging expeditions. Titmice are known to store seeds and nuts in the interstices of tree bark during fall and winter, often shelling them beforehand to allow for easy meals in the colder days ahead. Individuals also tend to select the largest seeds that will fit in their beaks, and peck them apart while pinning them to a perch with their feet. Song is a pellucid, high-whistled series of *pe-ter*, *pe-ter*, *pe-ter*, and calls include nasal buzzes and rasps similar to those of chickadees.

MIGRATE? No.

NESTING: Cavity nester. Uses tree hollows and former woodpecker nests, as well as small manmade cavities. A messy cup of grasses, mosses, and occasionally snake skins is constructed inside, and lined with animal hairs. About 4 in. wide.

EGGS: Off-white, with red or brown speckling. Length of ¾ in. Total of 3-8, sometimes with a second brood.

BIRD FEEDING TIPS

FEEDER DIET: Black-oil and hulled sunflower seeds, peanuts and peanut hearts, safflower seed, suet, mealworms. **FEEDER TYPES**: Platforms, hoppers, tubes, suet cages. **FEEDER BEHAVIOR**: Rarely stays for more than a few seconds during each visit, quickly finding a choice tidbit to store or consume nearby. Also, may use nest boxes.

COMPARE TO SIMILAR SPECIES: Black-crested Titmouse of Texas has a conspicuous, isolated dark crest. Much smaller and paler than Eastern Bluebird, with a fully white underside.

DID YOU KNOW? With the help of bird feeders, this species has expanded its original, more southerly range to include much of the Great Lakes and Northeast.

J F M A M J J A S O N D

240

Adults at top and bottom.

Adults at top and bottom.

① **WILLOW FLYCATCHER.** *Empidonax traillii.*

SIZE: 5 ¾ in.

HABITAT: Thickets and overgrown fields, normally near water.

WILD DIET: Insects. Sometimes, small fruits and berries in colder weather.

BEHAVIOR: Often observed on an outer branch of a thick shrub, occasionally vacating its perch to hunt for flying insects; insects on bushes and leaves may also be nabbed by briefly hovering. Does not usually return to the same perch, but may find a similar perch nearby. Known to flick its tail and wings rapidly while perched. In May and June, its peak breeding months, this species frequently sings loudly from elevated perches in its territory.

MIGRATE? Yes.

NESTING: Selects a low fork of a shrub or sapling, in which a cup-shaped nest is constructed. Neatly woven and anchored to branches with fine grasses. About 4 in. across and 3 in. high.

EGGS: Off-white, with some rufous speckling. Length of ¾ in. Total of 3-5.

FEEDER BEHAVIOR: Does not visit feeders.

COMPARE TO SIMILAR SPECIES: This species is a member of the *Empidonax* flycatchers, a group which also includes the Acadian, Alder, Least, and Yellow-bellied Flycatchers. All are of similar coloration and size, and nearly indistinguishable by sight in the field. However, each has a very different song, and prefers a different habitat (though this can be less reliable during spring migration). The Willow emits a quick, high, and raspy "fitz-bew" call; the "fitz" is ascending, and the "bew" descending.

DID YOU KNOW? Such is the difficulty in differentiating the *Empidonax* flycatchers that the Willow was consistently grouped with the Alder Flycatcher until the late 20th Century, with the given common name of Traill's Flycatcher.

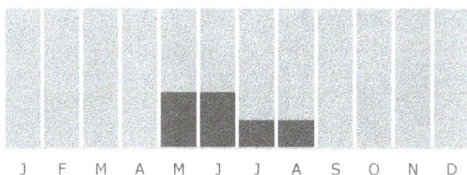

J F M A M J J A S O N D

(5) SONG SPARROW. *Melospiza melodia.*

SIZE: 5 ¾ in.

HABITAT: Thickets, hedgerows, overgrown fields, wetlands, open woods, parks. Very common in suburbs.

WILD DIET: Seeds (e.g., of grasses), fruits and berries, grains, insects and spiders.

BEHAVIOR: The most common sparrow across much of North America, this small, streaked species is ordinarily found skulking about brushy sections of habitat. In spring, the male spectacularly sings from exposed perches in bushes and small trees, with more exacting refrains preferred by potential female mates. Song is a sweet, multi-phrase melody of chips, whistles, buzzes, and trills.

MIGRATE? Partially.

NESTING: Usually placed on the ground in brushy or grassy areas, sometimes in a garden. Nest is cup-shaped, and woven with fine grasses. About 5-7 in. wide.

EGGS: Shades of blue-green, with brown speckling. Length of ¾ in. Total of 2-5, with 2-3 broods.

BIRD FEEDING TIPS

FEEDER DIET: Millet, milo, black-oil and hulled sunflower seeds, nyjer, peanut hearts, cracked corn, safflower seed, suet. **FEEDER TYPES**: Ground, platforms, hoppers, tubes. **FEEDER BEHAVIOR**: Very common on the ground beneath feeders, where it may take refuge in nearby cover between foraging sessions. Well-planted yards usually attract more individuals.

COMPARE TO SIMILAR SPECIES: Very similar to the Savannah Sparrow, which is instead found in open fields. May also resemble the Lincoln's Sparrow, which has a bolder topmost head stripe and a yellow tinge to the breast. Compared to female House and Purple Finches, this species has cleaner underside streaking and a less stout bill.

DID YOU KNOW? Song Sparrows successfully diminish the risks of predation and cowbird parasitism on their ground-based nests by laying several clutches of eggs throughout the late spring and summer.

J F M A M J J A S O N D

Adults at top and bottom.

Adult male at top,
Adult female at bottom (Photo by Fyn Kynd / CC BY-SA / Cropped).

② PURPLE FINCH. *Haemorhous purpureus.*

SIZE: 5 ¾ in.

HABITAT: Variety of woods, but favors conifers. Also, suburbs.

WILD DIET: Seeds, buds, berries, and insects.

BEHAVIOR: This cranberry-hued species actively forages by gleaning seeds and berries from foliage, occasionally landing on the ground to investigate fallen items of interest. Hops, rather than walks: like most other small finches and sparrows.

MIGRATE? Yes.

NESTING: Selects a sheltered spot in the outer branches of a tree, usually an evergreen. Cup-shaped, and woven with twigs and fine grasses. About 6-8 in. across.

EGGS: Light turquoise, with light brown speckling. Length of ¾ in. Total of 3-5, with 1-2 broods.

BIRD FEEDING TIPS

FEEDER DIET: Black-oil and hulled sunflower seeds, millet, nyjer. **FEEDER TYPES**: Platforms, ground, hoppers, tubes. **FEEDER BEHAVIOR**: May join larger flocks of House Finches. Substantial plantings of evergreens further attract this species.

COMPARE TO SIMILAR SPECIES: Purple Finch males have little to no streaking on the lower belly and have darker red coloration that runs from the head *into the wings and back*; females have *a pronounced pale eyebrow*. By contrast, House Finches generally have a dirtier, more heavily streaked lower belly and a more shallowly forked tail; in addition, males have no red on the wings and females lack well-defined striping across the side of head. Sparrows generally have daintier bills.

DID YOU KNOW? Though Purple Finches are only ordinarily found in the northern states and in Canada, they are known to irrupt southward across the U.S. during years of evergreen cone scarcity. In exceptional cases, it is likely that this species may even venture into Mexico in search of adequate food sources.

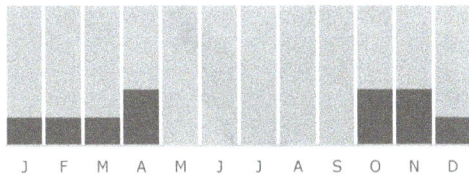

J F M A M J J A S O N D

② **EASTERN WOOD-PEWEE.** *Contopus virens.*

SIZE: 5 ½ in.

HABITAT: Variety of woods, but most frequently open, deciduous woods or edges of woods.

WILD DIET: Insects. Rarely, small fruits and berries.

BEHAVIOR: Selects elevated, well-visible perches from which to repeatedly sally out into the open for flying insects (e.g., dragonflies, wasps), occasionally stooping to vegetation or near the ground for wingless insects. Returns to the same perch after each flight; if an insect has been caught, it is repeatedly bludgeoned against the perch until it has been readied for consumption. Often hunts in the mid-canopy, beneath the domain of the Great Crested Flycatcher, but above that of the Least Flycatcher. Well-known for its ascending, high-whistled *pee-a-weee* call, which is sometimes audible for hundreds of feet.

MIGRATE? Yes.

NESTING: Nests at the confluence of several branches, about 30-60 ft. high. Finely woven cup of dried grasses and plant fibers. About 2 in. across.

EGGS: Off-white, with some rufous speckling. Length of ¾ in. Total of 2-4.

FEEDER BEHAVIOR: Does not visit feeders.

COMPARE TO SIMILAR SPECIES: To separate from *Empidonax* flycatchers, note that this species returns frequently to the same, conspicuous perch, and seldom flicks its tail. Possesses more defined white wing bars and an often sleeker silhouette than the Eastern Phoebe. Overall, characteristic song is highly diagnostic, especially when distinguishing from the Western Wood-Pewee in the Great Plains states.

DID YOU KNOW? Male wood-pewees aggressively defend a breeding territory of about 10 acres, and sometimes father two nests—each with a different female.

J F M A M J J A S O N D

Adults at top and bottom.

Adults at top and bottom.

① **FIELD SPARROW.** *Spizella pusilla.*

SIZE: 5 ½ in.

HABITAT: Brushy grasslands, overgrown fields, edges of woods, and orchards. Rarely, suburbs.

WILD DIET: Seeds (e.g., of grasses), insects and spiders.

BEHAVIOR: This species is a timorous, furtive sparrow of overgrown, rural grasslands. A common foraging habit consists of pouncing on long grasses, pinning the uppermost seed head, and picking it apart with its bill. Insects and spiders may also be snatched opportunistically in warmer months, particularly for the feeding of hatchlings (as is the case with many birds). In the breeding season, males territorially sing from nearby elevated perches, such as posts and apices of shrubs and trees; this melody is a series of high, clipped whistles which gradually accelerate to a trill.

MIGRATE? Partially.

NESTING: Selects a location on the ground or in a low fork of shrub. A bowl of dried grasses features wide, fading edges, which anchor the nest to nearby vegetation. Overall, about 8-10 in. across.

EGGS: Off-white, with brown speckling. Length of ¾ in. Total of 2-5. Usually raises 2 broods each year, but sometimes attempts to raise a third.

BIRD FEEDING TIPS

FEEDER DIET: Millet, hulled sunflower seeds, cracked corn, milo. **FEEDER TYPES**: Ground, platforms, hoppers. **FEEDER BEHAVIOR**: Very uncommon feeder visitor, and usually only in rural areas or during migratory periods. May be outcompeted by other sparrow species in mixed flocks.

COMPARE TO SIMILAR SPECIES: Similar to the breeding Chipping Sparrow, but note the Chipping's black eyeline and white eyebrow. In addition, the American Tree Sparrow is larger and much plumper, and is only present in colder months.

DID YOU KNOW? Field Sparrows are prodigious architects, building a new nest for each successive brood raised over the course of a given year.

J F M A M J J A S O N D

⑤ HOUSE FINCH. *Carpodacus mexicanus*.

SIZE: 5 ½ in.

HABITAT: Cities and suburbs, open woods.

WILD DIET: Grains, seeds, and berries.

BEHAVIOR: Forages for food on the ground or in shrubbery, and perches in trees. Readily adapts to human habitation, often flocking in the vicinity of known feeders. Sings with complex, warbling melodies; calls with a sharp, ascending, and yanking tone.

MIGRATE? No.

NESTING: Openings in buildings, in shrubs or trees, or in outdoor décor. Cup-shaped; formed from small twigs and debris. About 6 in. across, and often 5-10 ft. above the ground.

EGGS: Off-white to light blue or green, with some dark speckling. Length of ¾ in. Total of 3-5, with 2-3 broods.

BIRD FEEDING TIPS

FEEDER DIET: Black-oil and hulled sunflower seeds, nyjer, safflower seed. **FEEDER TYPES**: Platforms, ground, hoppers, tubes. **FEEDER BEHAVIOR**: Can accumulate in flocks of several dozen, jostling for position but remaining present for several minutes or more. May outcompete other species when found in sufficient numbers.

COMPARE TO SIMILAR SPECIES: Purple Finch males have little to no streaking on the lower belly and have darker red coloration that runs from the head into wings and back; females have a pronounced pale eyebrow. By contrast, House Finches generally have a dirtier, more heavily streaked lower belly and a more shallowly forked tail; in addition, males have *no red on the folded wings* and females *lack well-defined striping across the side of head*. Sparrows generally have daintier bills.

DID YOU KNOW? House Finches are only native to the western half of the U.S. Following illegal sales in the pet trade during the 1940s, they colonized the entire eastern U.S., working their way westward from New York City before finally reuniting with their relatives near the Rocky Mountains around the year 2000.

J F M A M J J A S O N D

Male at top,
Female at bottom.

Adults at top and bottom.

① NORTHERN ROUGH-WINGED SWALLOW.
Stelgidopteryx serripennis.

SIZE: 5 ½ in.

HABITAT: Semi-open country, usually near rivers, ponds, and lakes.

WILD DIET: Flying or aquatic insects (e.g., midges, mayflies, mosquitoes).

BEHAVIOR: This species flies over the water with strong, straight wingbeats, hawking for a variety of flying insects. Occasionally, individuals will also swoop for an assault on the water's surface, taking such invertebrates as water spiders. Less likely to flock than other swallow species, but may be found in interspecific flights during migratory events.

MIGRATE? Yes.

NESTING: Burrow nester, using tunnels excavated from sandy banks in past years by other species, such as Belted Kingfishers or Bank Swallows. May nest near the edge of an existing Bank Swallow colony. A stack-like cup is woven with grasses and reeds to fit the width of the chamber, which may be about 2 ft. deep.

EGGS: White to off-white. Length of ¾ in. Total of 3-8.

FEEDER BEHAVIOR: Does not visit feeders.

COMPARE TO SIMILAR SPECIES: Most similar in size, coloration, and profile to the Bank Swallow. Key differences include the Bank's dark breast band, and forked tail in flight (unlike the Northern Rough-winged's squared-off or rounded tail). In addition, silhouette and hunting behavior differ from those of flycatchers.

DID YOU KNOW? Northern Rough-winged Swallows are named for the finely serrated edge present on their outer wings, which feels gravelly if one were to run a finger across the margin. This species and its Latin American counterpart, the Southern Rough-winged, are the only swallows to feature this distinctive physical characteristic, though ornithologists have yet to discover its specific purpose.

J F M A M J J A S O N D

② **LEAST SANDPIPER.** *Calidris minutilla.*

SIZE: 5 ½ in.

HABITAT: Mudflats on edges of lakes, rivers, ponds, wetlands, and flooded fields.

WILD DIET: Insects and insect larvae, as well as very small aquatic invertebrates (e.g., snails).

BEHAVIOR: Probes the mud for small prey items buried in the substrate. Though it prefers mudflats, it also enters the inch-deep shallows of nearby water. Found in small to medium-sized groups, and may flock with other similarly sized shorebirds. Easily flushed if approached too closely, with individuals taking a somewhat direct path to another nearby foraging site. Along with the Spotted Sandpiper, this species is among the most common of all inland shorebirds.

MIGRATE? Yes.

NESTING: Breeds in the far north of Canada and Alaska. Forms a cuplike depression among stalks of thick grasses. About 2-3 in. across.

EGGS: Off-white with brown mottling. Length of 1 in. Total of 3-4.

FEEDER BEHAVIOR: Does not visit feeders.

COMPARE TO SIMILAR SPECIES: Other small "peep" sandpipers are often similar, but the Least is smallest and has *yellow legs.* Among breeding adults, the brown of its folded wings, back, and head cap is darker than that of the Semipalmated Sandpiper. Nonbreeding adults have a buffy band across the entire width of the breast and feature a darker gray-brown back, unlike the pale gray of the Western Sandpiper or the medium gray of the Semipalmated.

DID YOU KNOW? Though the smallest shorebird in the world, some individuals of this species have been known to undertake nonstop migratory flights exceeding 2,000 miles.

J F M A M J J A S O N D

Breeding adults at top,
Nonbreeding adults at bottom.

Breeding adult at top,
Nonbreeding adult at bottom.

⑤ CHIPPING SPARROW. *Spizella passerina.*

SIZE: 5 ½ in.

HABITAT: Open woods, parks, cities and suburbs.

WILD DIET: Seeds (e.g., of dandelions, wild buckwheat), insects and spiders.

BEHAVIOR: This spirited sparrow of the suburbs is ubiquitous in its favored habitat: hopping along near edges of lawns, perching in trees and shrubs, and gathering in small, loose flocks near feeders. Often prefers to perch between foraging sessions in sheltered, dense evergreens, if available. Song is a series of chipped, almost insect-like trills, which lasts up to five or six seconds.

MIGRATE? Yes.

NESTING: Selects a chest-high fork of branches in a shrub or tree, usually an evergreen. Height may be as low as one foot—or as high as 15 feet—above the ground. A cup is woven of twigs, grasses, and rootlets. About 5 in. across.

EGGS: Light blue or off-white, with brown spotting. Length of ¾ in. Total of 2-6, with 2 broods.

BIRD FEEDING TIPS

FEEDER DIET: Millet, milo, nyjer, hulled sunflower seeds. **FEEDER TYPES**: Hoppers, tubes, platforms, ground. **FEEDER BEHAVIOR**: Very common feeder visitor, and may also nest in a backyard tree or hedgerow. Gathers for moderate periods on smaller feeders, and may also loiter on the ground if fallen seed is present.

COMPARE TO SIMILAR SPECIES: During the breeding season, this species' rufous crest resembles that of the Field Sparrow, but note the black eyeline and long, white eyebrow of the Chipping (in addition to the fact that the Field is more common in open, rural grasslands).

DID YOU KNOW? Like many other birds, this species migrates by night—and, in fact, ranks as one of the most common such migrants. Ornithological sound technicians have been able to deduce species frequency patterns at a given site by counting nocturnal flight calls; usually, about 10 brief, high-pitched chips per hour can be easily heard for this species, and occasionally over 150 Chipping Sparrows per hour are logged.

J F M A M J J A S O N D

② **RED-EYED VIREO.** *Vireo olivaceus.*

SIZE: 5 ½ in.

HABITAT: Mature, old-growth, usually deciduous woods. During migration, also in open woods, parks, and suburbs.

WILD DIET: Mostly insects (e.g., caterpillars, flies) and spiders, but also fruits and berries (particularly before and during migration).

BEHAVIOR: This prodigious melodist is capable of generating numerous ditties over the course of a day, usually from high in a mature, deciduous tree. Individuals tend to move more purposefully than many of the warblers and kinglets, with short investigatory hops along the branches of the canopy. Smaller insects are quickly snapped up, while caterpillars and grasshoppers may be pinned to the perch with one claw while consumed piecemeal. Occasionally, vireos may hover near the tips of branches to capture elusive insects on the undersides of foliage. Songs consist of short, up-and-down series of chirped or murmured notes, often repeated after a rest of no more than a few seconds.

MIGRATE? Yes.

NESTING: Selects a location in a deciduous tree, with branches or twigs forming part of the nest's rim. Nest hangs from these anchor points, and is partially suspended in midair. Woven with grasses and twigs, and thoroughly bound with spider webbing. About 3 in. across.

EGGS: White, with fine spotting. Length of ¾ in. Total of 2-4, with 1-2 broods.

FEEDER BEHAVIOR: Does not visit feeders.

COMPARE TO SIMILAR SPECIES: Very similar to other vireo species, such as the Warbling and Philadelphia. Note the dark-outlined, clearly defined pale eyebrow, which is most prominent in the Red-eyed, as well as the contrast between its grey head cap and light green back.

DID YOU KNOW? Red-eyed Vireos may sing as many as 50 distinct songs, and rarely cease vocalizing: with some birds singing over 20,000 times in a single day.

J F M A M J J A S O N D

Adults at top and bottom.

Adult male at top (Note the black—rather than gray—cap),
Adult female at bottom.

④ WHITE-BREASTED NUTHATCH.
Sitta carolinensis.

SIZE: 5 ¼ in.

HABITAT: Mature woods, either open or dense. Also, parks and suburbs.

WILD DIET: Insects (e.g., ants, larvae, caterpillars) and spiders, seeds and nuts.

BEHAVIOR: Nuthatches are often observed clinging upside-down to tree bark, periodically extending their heads outward to survey their surroundings. Short, firm hops allow individuals to descend the tree trunk or cling to branches, often in search of insects (in the summer) or seeds and nuts (winter). Throughout the colder months, often observed in larger mixed flocks with titmice and chickadees, which assist with locating food sources and maintaining a vigil for lurking predators: particularly Cooper's and Sharp-shinned Hawks. Also known for its raucous, nasally, and cackling *ha-a-a-a-a...* calls, which may echo for hundreds of feet.

MIGRATE? No, but short movements may sometimes occur in winter.

NESTING: Cavity nester. Uses natural tree hollows or former woodpecker nests, which can be rather more commodious than one might expect. A bowl of grasses and bark is lined with feathers. About 4-5 in. across.

EGGS: White, with russet spotting. Length of ¾ in. Total of 3-8.

BIRD FEEDING TIPS

FEEDER DIET: Black-oil and hulled sunflower seeds, peanuts and peanut hearts, suet, mealworms, safflower seed. **FEEDER TYPES**: Tubes, hoppers, suet cages, platforms. **FEEDER BEHAVIOR**: A series of brief visits allows this species to take large seeds and nuts, before pecking them apart (or "hatching" them) in the cranny of a tree; these may also be stored in bark crevices in late fall and winter. Also, sometimes uses nest boxes.

COMPARE TO SIMILAR SPECIES: Red-breasted Nuthatch is very similar, but has a dark black eyeline and orange underside. Chickadees may also resemble this species, but note the distinct differences in movement (i.e., rarely upside down).

DID YOU KNOW? Nuthatches roost alone in tree cavities; however, in very cold weather, up to a couple dozen may crowd together in a single roost for warmth.

J F M A M J J A S O N D

③ **CHIMNEY SWIFT.** *Chaetura pelagica.*

SIZE: 5 ¼ in.

HABITAT: Cities and suburbs, parks, and fields.

WILD DIET: Flying insects (e.g., flies, ants, beetles, wasps).

BEHAVIOR: Usually described as a "cigar with wings," this diminutive bird spends the entire day in the air. Low wing-loading allows for seemingly effortless flight: with alternating gliding and flitting of wings, and calls which resound with a barrage of chittering. May reach diving speeds of well over 100 mph, and typically observed at speeds of 30 to 75 mph in level flight. During breeding season, most swifts stay relatively close to colonial nest sites, though individuals may venture up to five miles away. Swifts are unable to perch, and exclusively cling vertically to hard surfaces at their roosting or nesting sites, which include the interiors of chimneys and hollowed-out tree trunks.

MIGRATE? Yes.

NESTING: Previously nested in caves and hollowed tree trunks; now, almost exclusively nests in uncovered chimney flues. Bowl of twigs is bound together and to the vertical surface with cement-like saliva. About 4 in. across.

EGGS: Bright white. Length of ¾ in. Total of 3-5.

FEEDER BEHAVIOR: Does not visit feeders.

COMPARE TO SIMILAR SPECIES: Short, stubby body and very long, narrow wings differentiate from various swallows and nightjars. Unlike bats, this species normally flies by light of day.

DID YOU KNOW? Particularly during migration, flocks of thousands of swifts often descend to a communal roost, such as a chimney or smokestack, en masse. This results in an enormous, funnel-like conglomeration which ranks among the most enrapturing spectacles in all of urban birdwatching.

J F M A M J J A S O N D

Adults at top and bottom.

Adult male at top,
Adult female at bottom left (Photo by Andrew Weitzel / CC BY-SA / Cropped),
Juvenile at bottom right.

③ YELLOW-RUMPED WARBLER.
Setophaga coronata.

SIZE: 5 ¼ in.

HABITAT: Open to semi-open woods. In winter, also suburbs, parks, and dunes.

WILD DIET: Mostly insects (e.g., beetles, caterpillars, aphids) and spiders. In winter, also fruits and berries (e.g., bayberry, juniper, poison ivy).

BEHAVIOR: An adaptable and varied forager, this species is known to plunder spider webs, catch flying insects which pass too close to an exposed perch, and cling to and probe the bark of trees—in addition to more customary warbler foraging habitats, such as hopping along and exploring branches. In winter, this species may consume copious amounts of berries, allowing it to stay much farther north than many other warblers. Song is a simple, burbling series.

MIGRATE? Yes.

NESTING: Selects a location atop a cluster of conifer branches. Twigs, grasses, and needles are used to loosely weave a cup-shaped nest. About 3-4 in. across.

EGGS: Off-white, with brown speckling. Length of ¾ in. Total of 3-5, occasionally with a second brood.

BIRD FEEDING TIPS

FEEDER DIET: Suet, mealworms, fruit, grape jelly, sugar water, black-oil and hulled sunflower seeds, peanut hearts. **FEEDER TYPES**: Hoppers, tubes, platforms, suet cages, nectar feeders, ground. **FEEDER BEHAVIOR**: An uncommon feeder visitor, this species is most likely to visit during migration or in winter. May be otherwise common in the backyard.

COMPARE TO SIMILAR SPECIES: Most similar to Magnolia and Yellow-throated Warblers. The Yellow-rumped has a conspicuous black mask, yellow rump, white belly (unlike the yellow belly of the Magnolia) and band of streaking across the breast (unlike the fully yellow throat and breast of the Yellow-throated).

DID YOU KNOW? The Yellow-rumped Warbler is split into two North American subspecies, the Myrtle and the Audubon's. Myrtle Warblers are pictured at left, and are more common east of the Rockies; while the Audubon's features a yellow (rather than white) throat, and is more common near the Rockies and in the West.

J F M A M J J A S O N D

③ **BLACK-CAPPED CHICKADEE.**
Poecile atricapillus.

SIZE: 5 ¼ in.

HABITAT: Various woods, parks, and suburbs. Range closely overlaps with that of the Carolina Chickadee at southern boundary, as pictured and described at left.

WILD DIET: Insects (caterpillars, larvae) and spiders, seeds, nuts, and berries.

BEHAVIOR: This high-spirited species is normally found in loose flocks, acrobatically clinging to branches while gleaning hard-to-reach foodstuffs. Insects are taken in short flights or directly from vegetation. Upon securing a nut or seed and flying to a secure perch, the object is pinned against a branch with the feet and broken with the bill. Call is a well-known *chick-a-dee-dee...*, with the number of *dees* increasing with the relative level of perceived danger.

MIGRATE? No.

NESTING: Cavity nesters, often using a self-excavated hollow. Inside, a cup is arranged of grasses, and lined with animal hair. Interior nest is about 4 in. wide.

EGGS: White, with reddish-brown spotting. Length of ½ in. Total of 3-8.

BIRD FEEDING TIPS

FEEDER DIET: Black-oil and hulled sunflower seeds, peanuts and peanut hearts, suet, mealworms, safflower seed, nyjer. **FEEDER TYPES**: Platforms, hoppers, tubes, suet cages. **FEEDER BEHAVIOR**: Visits for no more than 10 seconds, and usually shorter—preferring to hull and consume seeds from nearby perch. Inquisitive. Occasionally uses nest boxes.

COMPARE TO SIMILAR SPECIES: Most similar to the slightly smaller Carolina Chickadee. Black-capped has much thicker white markings on its flight feathers, which are clearly observable across the side of the bird when its wings are folded; while the Carolina has finer, whitish-grey lines on its folded wings. The Boreal Chickadee of the northernmost U.S. has a brown cap and tawny flanks.

DID YOU KNOW? Like titmice, a group of chickadees is known as a banditry—owing either to their vaguely felonious black masks, or their snatch-and-grab feeding behavior.

J F M A M J J A S O N D

Adults at top and bottom,
Species range map inset (Note: Tan highlighting represents range of Black-capped Chickadee, and Black-capped/Carolina overlap zone occurs within a 25-mile-wide band north of the green area).

Adults at top and bottom.

⑤ CAROLINA WREN. *Thryothorus ludovicianus*.

SIZE: 5 ¼ in.

HABITAT: Thickets and thicketed woods, overgrown fields, and brushy suburbs and parks.

WILD DIET: Mostly insects (e.g., beetles, grasshoppers) and spiders. Occasionally, small reptiles and amphibians, or seeds and berries.

BEHAVIOR: This large, loquacious wren is a well-known fixture of many eastern North American landscapes. More often heard than seen, it forages near to the ground amid dense cover—though it may occasionally be observed singing from an exposed perch. Its calls and songs are heard many hundreds, or even thousands, of times each day; these sweet, chattering, and whistled tunes may sound like *tea-kettle, tea-kettle, tea-kettle* or *chippery, chippery, chippery*.

MIGRATE? No.

NESTING: Cavity nester. Adaptive in its selection of cavity, with known locations including tree hollows, as well as flowerpots, mailboxes, or other artificial items. Nest cup features a partial arched roof, and is constructed with dried grasses and leaves. About 5 in. across, on average.

EGGS: White, with rusty speckling. Length of ¾ in. Total of 3-6, with 2-3 broods.

BIRD FEEDING TIPS

FEEDER DIET: Suet, mealworms, peanut hearts, black-oil and hulled sunflower seeds.
FEEDER TYPES: Platforms, suet cages, hoppers, tubes, ground. **FEEDER BEHAVIOR**: Uncommon visitor. May be observed taking suet from cages, or mealworms from small platform cups. Uses nest boxes and specially designed wren houses.

COMPARE TO SIMILAR SPECIES: Bold, white eyebrow and tawny chest best distinguish from most other wrens.

DID YOU KNOW? The Carolina Wren is the official state bird of South Carolina, and was even featured on the Palmetto State's special-edition quarter. This coin was minted in 2000 as the eighth of 50 state quarters to enter general circulation.

J F M A M J J A S O N D

③ **INDIGO BUNTING.** *Passerina cyanea.*

SIZE: 5 ¼ in.

HABITAT: Mostly thickets and overgrown fields. Sometimes, edges of woods and roadsides; during migration, also suburbs, meadows, and open woods.

WILD DIET: Insects, seeds, berries, and grains.

BEHAVIOR: Forages low or along the ground in thickets, variably clinging to unstable stems and grasses as it cranes its neck to reach potential food sources. Normally found solitarily or in very small groups, aside from during migration. When singing (sometimes from elevated perches), note its high-pitched, coupled *whip*, *whip* or *chew*, *chew*, which forms the basis of longer melodic stanzas.

MIGRATE? Yes.

NESTING: Low to the ground, in a fork of dense vegetation. Cup-shaped, woven with grasses, and wrapped with spider webbing. About 2-3 in. across.

EGGS: White, sometimes with light brown spotting. Length of ¾ in. Total of 3-4, with 2 broods.

BIRD FEEDING TIPS

FEEDER DIET: Nyjer, millet, mealworms, milo, black-oil and hulled sunflower seeds, oats. **FEEDER TYPES**: Ground, tubes, hoppers, platforms. **FEEDER BEHAVIOR**: Most likely to visit in migration: sporadically in flocks of up to several dozen. Otherwise, uncommon.

COMPARE TO SIMILAR SPECIES: Key year-round differences from Lazuli Bunting of western North America include an absence of orange on the male's breast, and the lack of distinct wing bars on female. The Blue Grosbeak is also similar in appearance, but is larger and has a much stouter bill.

DID YOU KNOW? Indigo Buntings are the Galileans of the avian kingdom. During migration, which is undertaken by night, individuals accurately navigate by referencing the positions of the stars, even adjusting as constellations move over the course of weeks, seasons, and years. Indeed, captive buntings are even known to experience confusion if deprived of the ability to see the celestial lights.

J F M A M J J A S O N D

Breeding male at top,
Nonbreeding male at bottom left,
Female at bottom right.

Adult male at top,
Adult female at bottom.

③ YELLOW WARBLER. *Setophaga petechia.*

SIZE: 5 ¼ in.

HABITAT: Thicketed woods near rivers, streams, and wetlands. Also, parks and suburbs, particularly during migration.

WILD DIET: Insects (e.g., caterpillars, beetles) and spiders.

BEHAVIOR: This brightly appointed warbler is most at home in and around wet thickets, hopping along branches as it gleans insects. Like other warblers, this species is fairly active, frequently moving from branch to branch as it forages. Song is a cheerful, whistled *sweet-sweet-sweet-sweet, I'm so-so-sweet.*

MIGRATE? Yes.

NESTING: Selects a deep fork of a shrub or tree. A cup-shaped nest is woven of grasses and stems, and extensively bound with spider webbing. The nest is lined with feathers or downy pollen. About 3-4 in. across.

EGGS: Off-white to light blue-green, with brown spotting. Length of ¾ in. Total of 3-5.

FEEDER BEHAVIOR: Rarely visits feeders.

COMPARE TO SIMILAR SPECIES: Compared to other similar warblers, such as the Orange-crowned, this species is the only one which is so uniformly bright yellow. In addition, the male features distinctive red streaking on the breast.

DID YOU KNOW? The Yellow Warbler is one of the only avian species which consistently recognizes and defends against the threat of Brown-headed Cowbirds, with a specialized alert call often given if one is noticed nearby. Furthermore, if a cowbird lays eggs in the warbler's nest, a new nest will be immediately constructed atop the former one: smothering the mixed nest. If this is repeated several times over the course of the breeding season, a multi-story stack of nests may even emerge.

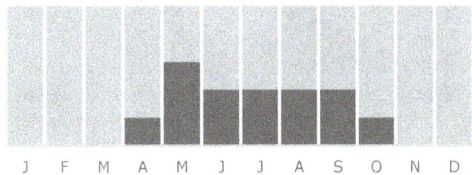

J F M A M J J A S O N D

275

④ TREE SWALLOW. *Tachycineta bicolor.*

SIZE: 5 in.

HABITAT: Fields, wetlands, and lakes.

WILD DIET: Mostly flying insects (e.g., dragonflies, ladybugs), sometimes egg shells and fish bones before egg-laying for added calcium. During cold snaps in its wintering range, may resort to consuming bayberries as well.

BEHAVIOR: Often observed perching on wires, branches, or fence posts, this species is common across its preferred habitat in most of North America. The Tree Swallow forages by gliding somewhat low over the ground, with occasional series of quick wingbeats to regain altitude and reorient its heading. Tends to flock more prolifically outside of breeding season, but loose groups may still be observed in the late spring to midsummer near optimal feeding sites. Calls are high-pitched, burbling, and echoing.

MIGRATE? Yes.

NESTING: Cavity nester. Uses a natural tree hollow, former woodpecker nest, or manmade nest box (sometimes a martin house); this site is usually close to water. Inside, a loose bowl is formed of dried grasses and aquatic reeds. About 4 in. wide.

EGGS: Bright white. Length of ¾ in. Total of 3-7.

FEEDER BEHAVIOR: Does not visit feeders, but does use nest boxes.

COMPARE TO SIMILAR SPECIES: Iridescent, blue-green back is highly distinctive among the North American swallows. Furthermore, this species is much smaller than the Purple Martin, and has a white, rather than dark, underside.

DID YOU KNOW? A single Tree Swallow may catch over one million flying insects in a single year, especially if feeding its hatchling young for a portion of the summer. When extrapolated to account for localized populations of several thousand individuals, one can easily see the extent to which this species is dependent on insect populations—which have fallen in the Tree Swallow's typical habitats by as much as one-half in the past 50 years.

J F M A M J J A S O N D

Adults at top and bottom.

Adults at top and bottom.

① WARBLING VIREO. *Vireo gilvus.*

SIZE: 5 in.

HABITAT: Mature, open, usually deciduous woods—including some parks and suburbs. Often found near water.

WILD DIET: Mostly insects (e.g., caterpillars, beetles, butterflies) and spiders, but also fruits and berries (particularly before and during migration).

BEHAVIOR: A bird of the treetops, the vireo is more often seen than heard; however, for many suburbanites in older-growth neighborhoods, this may occur on a relatively frequent basis. This species hops along the branches, gleaning insects from the undersides of leaves, and occasionally resorts to hover-snatching for more elusive prey. Likely to aggressively guard nests from ovivorous, or egg-eating, predators. Like many vireos, males sing all throughout the day in spring and summer. Their song lasts a few seconds, consists of a series of up-and-down burbles and slurs, and is usually repeated after a few seconds' pause.

MIGRATE? Yes.

NESTING: Selects a location in a deciduous tree, with two intersecting branches forming part of the nest's rim. The nest is suspended from these anchor points, and takes the shape of a deep, hanging cup. Constructed with grasses and plant fibers, and tightly bound with spider silk. About 3 in. wide.

EGGS: White, with fine spotting. Length of ¾ in. Total of 2-4, with 1-2 broods.

FEEDER BEHAVIOR: Does not visit feeders.

COMPARE TO SIMILAR SPECIES: Very similar to other vireos, such as the Red-eyed and Philadelphia. The rounded, less boldly defined eyebrow distinguishes from Red-eyed, while the lack of bright yellow on the central underside differentiates from the Philadelphia. Warblers, such as the Tennessee, have a much thinner bill.

DID YOU KNOW? Vireos have lost well over half of their total populations in the past century, primarily due to the increasing usage of herbicides and pesticides.

J F M A M J J A S O N D

② PALM WARBLER. *Setophaga palmarum.*

SIZE: 5 in.

HABITAT: Open woods, overgrown fields, wetland edges. During migration, also parks and suburbs.

WILD DIET: Insects (e.g., beetles, flies) and spiders. In winter, sometimes berries.

BEHAVIOR: This warbler commonly hunts for insects along the ground or low in shrubs, merrily bobbing its tail as it walks or hops along. Individuals may select an exposed perch and chase after nearby flying insects. Not ordinarily found in groups during the warmer months, but may form larger mixed flocks with sparrows and other warblers on its wintering grounds. Song is a mechanical, monotonous, and rattling trill similar to that of the Chipping Sparrow.

MIGRATE? Yes.

NESTING: Breeds in northern coniferous forests; it selects a nesting location on the ground, at the base of a fern or shrub. A roughly hewn bowl of twigs and plant fibers is assembled. About 4-5 in. wide.

EGGS: White, with light brown blotches. Length of ¾ in. Total of 4-5, with 2 broods.

FEEDER BEHAVIOR: Rarely visits feeders.

COMPARE TO SIMILAR SPECIES: Most similar to the less common Prairie Warbler, which lacks the rufous head crown of the breeding Palm Warbler, as well as the pale eyebrow of the nonbreeding Palm.

DID YOU KNOW? The Palm Warbler's common name can be misleading, as individuals seldom associate with palm trees in their natural habitat. This name was given in 1789 by the German naturalist J.P. Gmelin, who located a wintering specimen on the Caribbean island of Hispaniola and subsequently named this warbler for the palms common to the surrounding area.

J F M A M J J A S O N D

Breeding adult at top,
Nonbreeding adult at bottom.

Adult above (Photo by Mdf / CC BY-SA / Cropped).

① **LEAST FLYCATCHER.** *Empidonax minimus.*

SIZE: 5 in.

HABITAT: Variety of woods, but usually open, mature woods with plenty of thickets.

WILD DIET: Insects. Sometimes, small fruits and berries in colder weather.

BEHAVIOR: Often on the move as it makes its way throughout the forest understory, flying between various perches (rarely returning directly to the same one) and hovering to grab insects from the air or vegetation. A feisty customer, individuals are known to repeatedly chase away other birds from claimed breeding territories. Sings repeatedly during mating season, mostly in May.

MIGRATE? Yes.

NESTING: Semicolonial, with about 150 ft. separating individual nests of Least Flycatcher pairs. Selects a fork in a tree, in which a woven cup of grasses is constructed. About 2 ½ in. across.

EGGS: White. Length of ½ in. Total of 3-5.

FEEDER BEHAVIOR: Does not visit feeders.

COMPARE TO SIMILAR SPECIES: This species is a member of the *Empidonax* flycatchers, a group which also includes the Acadian, Alder, Willow, and Yellow-bellied Flycatchers. All are of similar coloration and size, and nearly indistinguishable by sight in the field. However, each has a very different song, and prefers a different habitat (though this can be less reliable during spring migration). The Least has a clipped, dry *che-beck* song; this lasts less than a quarter-second and may be repeated many times in relatively quick succession.

DID YOU KNOW? The smaller size and bold, white eye-ring of this species make it perhaps the most identifiable *Empidonax* flycatcher for novices, particularly during migration. In these months, many flycatchers are less discerning in their choice of habitat, thus nullifying what is normally a helpful differentiator. The *Empidonax* genus—of which the Least Flycatcher is a member—is host to a total of 11 North American species, many of which are nearly identical at a passing glance.

J F M A M J J A S O N D

① **BROWN CREEPER.** *Certhia americana.*

SIZE: 5 in.

HABITAT: Mature woods, both semi-open and dense. Often prefers conifers.

WILD DIET: Mostly insects and spiders; sometimes seeds in winter.

BEHAVIOR: The small stature and drab, well-camouflaged coloration of this tree-clinging species often make it difficult to spot—particularly when considering that it inhabits thicker, more mature tracts of woodland. However, this species' unique decurved bill and upward-spiraling hopping motion remain a distinct treat for any observer. The Brown Creeper frequently starts at the bottom of a tree, moving all the way to the top before repeating this pattern on a nearby tree. Additionally, the long, stiff tail acts like a brace when clinging to trees, similar to the behavior observed in woodpeckers, while its unusual bill is particularly adept at chiseling into the bark for insects. Its voice is typically thin, *seet*-like, and high-pitched.

MIGRATE? Yes.

NESTING: Selects a decaying opening in the tree bark, or a spot wedged between an extended bark slab and the trunk. Twigs, leaves, and grasses form a small cup nestled against the trunk. About 3-4 in. across.

EGGS: White, with reddish-brown spotting. Length of ½ in. Total of 4-7.

BIRD FEEDING TIPS

FEEDER DIET: Suet, peanut hearts, hulled sunflower seeds. **FEEDER TYPES**: Suet cages, tubes. **FEEDER BEHAVIOR**: Uncommon feeder visitor, and normally only takes suet.

COMPARE TO SIMILAR SPECIES: Most similar to the nuthatches, but upward movement along the trunk—as well as general appearance—is distinctive.

DID YOU KNOW? Referencing its especial climbing motion, a group of creepers is known as a spiral (e.g., a spiral of creepers).

J F M A M J J A S O N D

Adults at top and bottom.

Adults at top and bottom.

① WHITE-EYED VIREO. *Vireo griseus.*

SIZE: 5 in.

HABITAT: Thickets, overgrown fields, edges of woods.

WILD DIET: Mostly insects (e.g., caterpillars) and spiders, but also fruits and berries (particularly in fall and winter).

BEHAVIOR: The fierce countenance of the White-eyed Vireo belies its tendency to associate with dense, enshrouding thickets. As such, it is often difficult to catch a glimpse of this bird in the open, and may be easiest to recognize by song. Individuals deliberately scramble and flitter about through the brush, seeking out hidden insects— particularly caterpillars. Song is a bouncy, chirped *spit-a-phooey-phooey-spit!*, with the *spit* notes sometimes harsh and raspy.

MIGRATE? Yes.

NESTING: Selects a location between two intersecting branches, which form part of the nest's rim. Nest is hung from these anchoring points, and is cup-shaped. Constructed with fine grasses and plant fibers, and bound with several layers of spider silk, which may give the nest a frosted appearance. About 2-3 in. wide.

EGGS: White, with fine, well-spaced, and dark spotting. Length of ¾ in. Total of 2-5, with 1-2 broods.

FEEDER BEHAVIOR: Does not visit feeders.

COMPARE TO SIMILAR SPECIES: Bright yellow spectacles, along with a pale throat and chest, differentiate from other vireos. To distinguish from warblers, particularly note the much stouter bill characteristic to the vireo family.

DID YOU KNOW? Like the Red-eyed Vireo, this species' eye color changes over the course of its first year. Juvenile White-eyeds originally have dark brown eyes, which gradually transition to feature a pale or white iris by the following spring.

J F M A M J J A S O N D

287

⑤ AMERICAN GOLDFINCH. *Spinus tristis*.

SIZE: 5 in.

HABITAT: Overgrown fields and meadows, suburbs, and parks.

WILD DIET: Seeds (e.g., thistle, sunflower, dandelion, milkweed, alder).

BEHAVIOR: An active, social, and often highly visible finch, this species tends to hopscotch from plant to plant as it meticulously gleans the seeds which constitute the near entirety of its diet—a dietary trait known as *granivory*. Can be quite nimble in hanging from flowers and other seed heads, allowing this bird to reach a number of food sources that would be otherwise inaccessible. Sings with a high tone and cadence of *po-ta-to-chip*, and calls most frequently with a high, yanking duplet of whistles.

MIGRATE? Partially. Some individuals move southward if temperatures dip below freezing, and particularly if below zero.

NESTING: Usually in shrubbery or hedgerows, well elevated off the ground. Small cup woven of plant fibers, and lined with downy pollen. Anchored to branches with spider webbing. About 3 in. across.

EGGS: Off-white to light blue, with light spotting. Length of ¾ in. Total of 2-6, occasionally with a second brood.

BIRD FEEDING TIPS

FEEDER DIET: Nyjer, black-oil and hulled sunflower seeds. **FEEDER TYPES**: Tubes, hoppers, platforms, ground. **FEEDER BEHAVIOR**: Very common at feeders, and tends to loiter in the same manner as House Finches. Molt can be gradually observed in early spring, transitioning from drab buff into bright yellow as it triumphantly enters its breeding season.

COMPARE TO SIMILAR SPECIES: Most similar to the smaller Lesser Goldfinch of the West and Southwest. Notable differences include the American's bright yellow (in breeding season) or pale back (nonbreeding), and orange bill (breeding). In addition, the Lesser rarely, if ever, occurs northeast of Missouri.

DID YOU KNOW? The American Goldfinch is the state bird of Iowa, New Jersey, and Washington.

J F M A M J J A S O N D

Breeding female at top,
Breeding male at bottom left,
Nonbreeding adult at bottom right.

Adult male at top,
Adult female at bottom.

② **AMERICAN REDSTART.** *Setophaga ruticilla.*

SIZE: 5 in.

HABITAT: Large tracts of semi-open woods, often with thickets and situated near water.

WILD DIET: Mostly insects (e.g., moths, flies, caterpillars) and spiders. In early fall, occasionally consumes berries and seeds.

BEHAVIOR: This boldly colored warbler with the show-stopping, fan-shaped tail gracefully flits like a butterfly throughout the forest understory. Somewhat uniquely for warblers, it catches most of its insects aerially with flycatcher-like sallies, though it also gleans directly from branches. When approaching a brushy area, individuals will often open or fan their tails, flushing any nearby insects with a bright flash of color. Song is a series of burry *zeets* and effervescent whistles.

MIGRATE? Yes.

NESTING: Situated in a vertical fork of tree branches, usually adjacent to the trunk. A cup is manufactured to conform to the fork, and is well-woven with fine plant fibers, often bound with lichens or the nest combs of paper wasps. About 3 in. across.

EGGS: Off-white, with heavy reddish-brown speckling. Length of ¾ in. Total of 2-5.

FEEDER BEHAVIOR: Does not visit feeders.

COMPARE TO SIMILAR SPECIES: The male Blackburnian Warbler has orange that is limited to the head and throat, contrasting with the male American Redstart's fully black head. This species' coloration is also similar to that of the Baltimore Oriole, but note the redstart's much smaller size and differing foraging habits.

DID YOU KNOW? In Jamaica, this species is commonly nicknamed the "latrine bird" for its partiality for hanging around outdoor toilets and garbage dumps. These sites predictably host a king's ransom of flies, which the wintering redstarts gleefully devour.

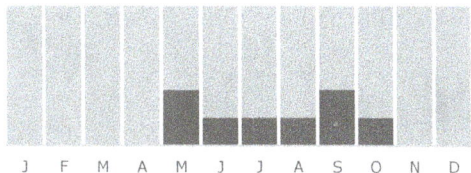

J F M A M J J A S O N D

291

① **PINE SISKIN.** *Spinus pinus*.

SIZE: 5 in.

HABITAT: Open woods, both coniferous and mixed. Also, suburbs and parks.

WILD DIET: Mostly seeds (e.g., from cones of conifers, dandelions, and wild grasses). Also, buds, stems, and insects and spiders.

BEHAVIOR: Often tucked away among the dense needles of conifers, darting from tree to tree as it pierces open seed pods, such as woody pine cones. May venture to ground level if fallen seeds or newfound sprouts appear. A somewhat opportunistic feeder, this species will nibble at leaves, stems, and even buds of garden vegetables if given the chance; it has also been known to eat the fallen pieces of seeds left by the foraging sessions of larger birds.

MIGRATE? Sometimes. In years with inadequate wild conifer cone yields, famished siskins move southward en masse.

NESTING: Concealed location in an outer fork of branches, often in a conifer. A slender-lipped bowl is woven of fine grasses, and lined with downy pollen or feathers. About 3-4 in. across.

EGGS: Light blue-green, with faint brown spotting. Length of ¾ in. Total of 3-5, occasionally with a second brood.

BIRD FEEDING TIPS

FEEDER DIET: Nyjer, black-oil and hulled sunflower seeds, suet. **FEEDER TYPES**: Tubes, hoppers, platforms, ground. **FEEDER BEHAVIOR**: May be somewhat common one year, and absent the next. Gregarious and genial. Attracted by extensive conifer plantings.

COMPARE TO SIMILAR SPECIES: May resemble a goldfinch, to whom this species is closely related, but the heavy streaking all across its body is very distinctive.

DID YOU KNOW? The Pine Siskin is well adapted to its typically northern environment. During winter nights, this species is able to survive temperatures as low as -100 °F by turning its fat-burning mechanisms into overdrive, and by converting large quantities of seeds stored in its throat pouch to thermal energy.

J F M A M J J A S O N D

Male at top (Notice heavy yellow on wings),
Female at bottom.

Adults at top and bottom.

③ HOUSE WREN. *Troglodytes aedon*.

SIZE: 4 ¾ in.

HABITAT: Open woods, thickets, suburbs, parks, and gardens.

WILD DIET: Insects (e.g., caterpillars, ladybugs) and spiders (e.g., daddy longlegs).

BEHAVIOR: This species busily forages in the brushy understory of open woodland, searching for small, terrestrial insects and spiders. It is highly adaptable to various habitats, so long as they feature some brush or nearby thicket. Song is a burbling and rattling series of notes, which is typically only repeated throughout the spring and summer; in the spring, males frequently sing from elevated perches to attract mates, while females also sing during the nesting season to assert their dominance over the immediate area.

MIGRATE? Yes.

NESTING: Cavity nester. Selects a natural cavity, former woodpecker nest, or artificial substitute. A thin cup of twigs and grasses is lined with feathers. About 3-4 in. across.

EGGS: Off-white to light pink, with light speckling. Length of ¾ in. Total of 4-8, with 2 broods.

BIRD FEEDING TIPS

FEEDER DIET: Mealworms, suet. **FEEDER TYPES**: Platforms. **FEEDER BEHAVIOR**: Rare visitor. Most attracted by small platform cups filled with mealworms or bits of suet. Also, may use nest boxes and specially designed wren houses.

COMPARE TO SIMILAR SPECIES: Most similar to the regionally uncommon Winter Wren, which has dark belly streaking and is somewhat darker overall.

DID YOU KNOW? House Wrens are quite aggressive with regard to their nests. They have been known to fill the nests of nearby wrens with sticks, and even puncture their eggs. In addition, if a suitable nest cavity has already been taken, the female may displace the incumbent pair to take the location for herself.

J F M A M J J A S O N D

③ COMMON YELLOWTHROAT. *Geothlypis trichas.*

SIZE: 4 ¾ in.

HABITAT: Thickets, often near wetlands or edges of woods. May be observed in less densely thicketed areas during migration.

WILD DIET: Insects (e.g., beetles, ants, flies) and spiders.

BEHAVIOR: This species is often found scrambling about the low branches of damp thickets as it undertakes its daily foraging activities. The male's roguish mask is one of the most recognizable features on a North American warbler, and functions as a signal of masculine territoriality to its conspecifics. Song is a high, warbled series of *twiddly-twiddly-twiddly...*, which is very noticeable as males establish and maintain their breeding territories in late spring and summer.

MIGRATE? Yes.

NESTING: Near the ground, amid marshy vegetation. Nest is cup-shaped, and woven of dried reeds and stems. About 4 in. across.

EGGS: Off-white to light blue-green, with brown markings. Length of ¾ in. Total of 3-5, with 2 broods.

FEEDER BEHAVIOR: Rarely visits feeders, usually for suet.

COMPARE TO SIMILAR SPECIES: Male's black mask is fairly distinctive. Females are best distinguished by the combination of their yellow throat and breast, white belly, and olive back.

DID YOU KNOW? Of the billions of birds which migrate across the Gulf of Mexico each year, many fail to complete the parlous journey. As a result, tiger sharks—widely recognized for their wide-ranging eating habits, including the consumption of cans and license plates—have learned to congregate in certain sections of ocean where birds are most likely to fall, and Common Yellowthroats have been positively identified in the stomach contents of several analyzed tiger sharks.

J F M A M J J A S O N D

Adult male at top,
Adult female at bottom.

Adult male at top (Note the black throat),
Adult female at bottom.

① BLACK-AND-WHITE WARBLER. *Mniotilta varia.*

SIZE: 4 ¾ in.

HABITAT: Wide variety of woods, including well-wooded suburbs.

WILD DIET: Insects (e.g., caterpillars, ants, beetles) and spiders.

BEHAVIOR: This species is rather unique among the warblers, in that it frequently forages by clinging to tree bark. This nuthatch-esque behavior can be quite entertaining to watch, with individuals often hanging from branches, scraping at bark, and generally making acrobats of themselves. To suit these eclectic habits, this species' toes—particularly the hind toe—are longer than other warblers', which allows for a secure grip on vertical surfaces. Throughout the spring and early summer, Black-and-whites primarily consume caterpillars, which may be located on the undersides of difficult-to-reach branches. Song is a high, quick, and repeated *wheezy, wheezy, wheezy.*

MIGRATE? Yes.

NESTING: Selects a concealed location on the ground. A wide-rimmed nest cup is constructed with leaves and grasses. About 4-5 in. wide.

EGGS: Off-white, with reddish speckling. Length of ¾ in. Total of 4-5, occasionally with a second brood.

FEEDER BEHAVIOR: Does not visit feeders.

COMPARE TO SIMILAR SPECIES: Most similar to the Blackpoll Warbler, which is also black and white. However, while the Black-and-white features a boldly striped head, the Blackpoll instead has a plain, black cap and a broad, white cheek.

DID YOU KNOW? While a flock of warblers is commonly known as a bouquet, wrench, or confusion, the Black-and-white has its own collective noun; ergo, a flock is known as a *dichotomy* of Black-and-white Warblers—referencing the rather binary coloration of its plumage.

J F M A M J J A S O N D

299

① **MAGNOLIA WARBLER.** *Setophaga magnolia.*

SIZE: 4 ¾ in.

HABITAT: Breeds in coniferous woods, but may be observed in a variety of woods during migration (including wooded suburbs and parks).

WILD DIET: Insects (e.g., caterpillars) and spiders.

BEHAVIOR: This caterpillar specialist prefers to forage in trees, searching for its prey on the undersides of branches. During courtship displays, males tend to flash the white-and-black underside of its tail, which is also readily observable by birders during overhead flyovers. The Magnolia's song is repeated throughout the day, but most common in twilight; the short, warbled, up-and-down tune sounds like *twiddle, twiddle, TWEEdle.*

MIGRATE? Yes.

NESTING: Selects a location in a conifer, sometimes near the trunk. Nest is a bulky cup of twigs and grasses. About 4 in. wide.

EGGS: Off-white, with reddish-brown splotching. Length of ¾ in. Total of 3-5.

FEEDER BEHAVIOR: Rarely visits feeders, usually for suet.

COMPARE TO SIMILAR SPECIES: For males, combination of black mask, white wing patch, and stringy black necklace are highly diagnostic. Females have a much weaker mask and necklace, and feature *two white wing bars*. Similar species include the Nashville and Canada Warblers.

DID YOU KNOW? The Magnolia Warbler was first identified by the famed ornithologist Alexander Wilson on a Mississippi nature expedition in 1810. He originally named it the Black-and-yellow Warbler, but the specific name of *magnolia*—also given by Wilson, for the tree in which the bird was perched—has grown to be its most common name.

J F M A M J J A S O N D

Adult male at top,
Adult female at bottom.

Adults at top and bottom,
Species range map inset (Note: Green highlighting represents range of Carolina Chickadee, and
Black-capped/Carolina overlap zone occurs within a 25-mile-wide band north of the green area).

(4) CAROLINA CHICKADEE. *Poecile carolinensis.*

SIZE: 4 ½ in.

HABITAT: Various woods, parks, and suburbs. Range closely overlaps with that of the Black-capped Chickadee at the northern edge, as pictured and described at left.

WILD DIET: Insects (caterpillars, larvae) and spiders, seeds, nuts, and berries.

BEHAVIOR: Large, loose flocks of this species often maraud open wooded areas, nimbly perching and hanging from branches. Gleaned nuts and seeds are pinned to a branch with the feet, and broken open with the bill. The familiar *chick-a-dee-dee...* call of this species is higher and quicker than that of the Black-capped; in addition, the number of *dees* increases with the level of perceived danger.

MIGRATE? No.

NESTING: Cavity nester (e.g., self-excavated, or existing hollow or nest cavity). Inside, a cup is fashioned with plant fibers and lined with animal fur. About 4 in. wide.

EGGS: White, with reddish-brown spotting. Length of ½ in. Total of 3-8.

BIRD FEEDING TIPS

FEEDER DIET: Black-oil and hulled sunflower seeds, peanuts and peanut hearts, suet, mealworms, safflower seed, nyjer. **FEEDER TYPES**: Platforms, hoppers, tubes, suet cages. **FEEDER BEHAVIOR**: Briefly visits, before carrying away its haul to a nearby perch. Inquisitive, and may even approach humans. Occasionally uses nest boxes.

COMPARE TO SIMILAR SPECIES: Most similar to the slightly larger Black-capped Chickadee. Carolina has much finer, white (almost greyish) lines on its wing feathers, which are observable across its side when the wings are folded. Contrastingly, the Black-capped has thicker, bolder white markings on its folded wings.

DID YOU KNOW? Where the ranges of the Black-capped and Carolina Chickadees overlap, such as in the Greater Pittsburgh area, the two species readily interbreed and hybridize. This overlap zone is moving northward at a rate of approximately 10 to 15 miles per decade—primarily due to the effects of rising global temperatures.

J F M A M J J A S O N D

① **NORTHERN PARULA.** *Setophaga americana.*

SIZE: 4 ½ in.

HABITAT: Mature, dense woods, often near water.

WILD DIET: Mostly insects (e.g., caterpillars, cicadas) and spiders. Occasionally, berries.

BEHAVIOR: The canopy-dwelling Northern Parula actively hops along branches as it forages, often targeting caterpillars and spiders. Wingbeats are quick as individuals fly between perches, making this bird seemingly appear as a blue flash as it bursts through gaps in the foliage. Like many warblers, this species tends to forage by itself or in pairs throughout much of the summer, and joins large, loose flocks during migration. Song is a buzzing trill, with a gradually rising glissando.

MIGRATE? Yes.

NESTING: Selects a high location amid hanging mosses or lichens (e.g., particularly Spanish moss, also Old Man's Beard lichen). Nest is an enclosed cup that is formed and hollowed out of a particularly thick clump of this hanging vegetation. About 4 in. wide.

EGGS: White, with red-brown spotting. Length of ¾ in. Total of 3-6, with 1-2 broods.

FEEDER BEHAVIOR: Does not visit feeders.

COMPARE TO SIMILAR SPECIES: This bird is impressively distinctive; notice the blue head and back, as well as the yellow throat and white belly.

DID YOU KNOW? The Northern Parula's penchant for treetop foraging has exacerbated many a case of *warbler neck*, a common orthopedic condition which temporarily causes stiffness of neck among birders. During migratory periods, when species diversity is often highest, many birders will crane their necks upwards for extended periods as they seek to build an impressive species count—an exercise which may be best accompanied by the application of an ice pack later in the day.

J F M A M J J A S O N D

Adult male at top (Note the thick, black throat band),
Adult female at bottom.

Adults at top and bottom.

② BLUE-GRAY GNATCATCHER.
Polioptila caerulea.

SIZE: 4 ½ in.

HABITAT: Open woods, often with thickets and sometimes near water.

WILD DIET: Insects (e.g., grasshoppers, insect larvae) and spiders.

BEHAVIOR: This petite insectivore is often observed spreading, flicking, or cocking its tail as it moves along through the foliage, a mechanism which may help to flush any nearby insects. Otherwise, its insect prey is gleaned by hovering near leaves or tips of branches, aerially hawking, or hopping along stems and branches. This species' vocalizations consist of a series of thin, almost electronic-sounding buzzes, which variably ascend and descend in pitch.

MIGRATE? Yes.

NESTING: Selects a location adjacent to a junction of branches. The nest takes the shape of a rounded cup; it is woven with grasses and stems, and thickly bound with spider silk, which also anchors the nest to the tree. Not reused. About 2-3 in. wide.

EGGS: Off-white, with reddish-brown spotting. Length of ½ in. Total of 3-6, with 1-2 broods.

FEEDER BEHAVIOR: Does not visit feeders.

COMPARE TO SIMILAR SPECIES: The only other gnatcatcher to reside in North America is the Black-tailed Gnatcatcher, which is uncommon along the U.S.-Mexico border; the Black-tailed features a prominent black head cap.

DID YOU KNOW? The gnatcatchers are the sole North American representatives of the *Sylviidae* family, which primarily includes the Old World (or Eurasian) warblers. Intriguingly, this family is entirely genetically distinct from the *Parulidae* family of North American warblers.

J F M A M J J A S O N D

① **RED-BREASTED NUTHATCH.** *Sitta canadensis.*

SIZE: 4 ½ in.

HABITAT: Mature woods, both open and dense. Prefers conifers. In winter, may visit parks and suburbs with more regularity.

WILD DIET: Insects (e.g., ants, beetles) and spiders, seeds and nuts.

BEHAVIOR: The large, muscular claws of this species allow it to descend headfirst down trunks of trees as it forages, sometimes veering to one side or the other. Gleaned insects and seeds are increasingly stored in crannies and crevices of the bark as winter approaches. When flying between trees, an undulating flight pattern is observable—with brisk, sturdy flaps of the wings occasionally allowing the individual to regain altitude. Song and calls are a higher-pitched series of yanking guffaws than those of the White-breasted, its close genetic relative.

MIGRATE? Sometimes, and to varying degrees. When conifer seed crops are lower than usual, wide-scale irruptions of this species move southward in search of food.

NESTING: Cavity nester. Usually self-excavates, but may also use existing tree hollows or cavities. Inside, a rough bowl of bark and twigs is lined with feathers. About 4-5 in. across.

EGGS: White, with russet spotting. Length of ¾ in. Total of 3-8.

BIRD FEEDING TIPS

FEEDER DIET: Black-oil and hulled sunflower seeds, peanuts and peanut hearts, suet, mealworms, safflower seed. **FEEDER TYPES**: Tubes, hoppers, suet cages, platforms. **FEEDER BEHAVIOR**: Often observed making a series of quick visits, before flying away to hatch or store its haul. May associate with chickadees or titmice. May also use nest boxes.

COMPARE TO SIMILAR SPECIES: White-breasted Nuthatch is very similar, but lacks *a dark black eyeline* and orange-hued underside. Chickadees may also resemble this species, but note the differences in movement (i.e., rarely upside down).

DID YOU KNOW? Nuthatches are named for their proclivity for breaking apart, or hatching, large nuts in the hardened crevices of trees.

J F M A M J J A S O N D

Adult male at top (Note the darker cap and underside),
Adult female at bottom.

Adults at top and bottom.

② **RUBY-CROWNED KINGLET.** *Regulus calendula.*

SIZE: 4 in.

HABITAT: Breeds in mature, coniferous woods. During migration, often found in a variety of woods or thickets, including parks and suburbs.

WILD DIET: Insects (e.g., flies, ants) and spiders. Occasionally, fruits and seeds.

BEHAVIOR: This small bird has an enormously high metabolism, forcing it to forage actively all throughout the day. These caffeinated foraging habits often consist of hopping along branches, hovering near tips of branches or leaves, and sallying out into swarms of flying insects. Though less likely to flock with other kinglets during the breeding season—and often behaving quite territorially, with males flicking their rarely observed red head crests at rivals—this species often mixes with hordes of warblers and chickadees during migratory or wintering periods. Song is a distinctive mix of *seets*, chirps, trills, and slurs.

MIGRATE? Yes. Some birds may also winter in this state.

NESTING: Selects a location in a conifer. Nest is cup-shaped, and suspended from two or three branches, which are woven into the walls or rim of the nest. Constructed with a mix of grasses and feathers, and bound with spider silk. About 3-4 in. wide.

EGGS: Dull white. Length of ½ in. Total of 4-12.

FEEDER BEHAVIOR: Rarely visits feeders, usually for suet.

COMPARE TO SIMILAR SPECIES: Most similar to the closely related Golden-crowned Kinglet, which instead features a striped face and a visible golden-yellow head crest.

DID YOU KNOW? Relative to size, the kinglets lay the most eggs of any North American bird species. Just before laying, up to three-quarters of the female's weight may be comprised of her eggs alone—a truly remarkable feat.

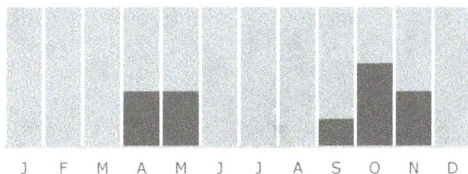

J F M A M J J A S O N D

311

① GOLDEN-CROWNED KINGLET.
Regulus satrapa.

SIZE: 3 ¾ in.

HABITAT: Breeds in coniferous woods. During migration and winter, may inhabit a variety of woods, including wooded parks and suburbs.

WILD DIET: Insects (e.g., flies, beetles, insect larvae) and spiders. Rarely, seeds.

BEHAVIOR: This highly active species is present in all levels of the forest, but most frequently in the canopy. Individuals forage by directly gleaning from branches, briefly hovering near clusters of leaves, and opportunistically flying into swarms of insects. The Golden-crowned is territorial in breeding season, but otherwise often associates in small groups with its fellow conspecifics or members of other species, such as chickadees, warblers, and titmice. Individuals may also be relatively tame around humans in some areas. This species' song is vaguely similar to the Ruby-crowned's, with a series of high, accelerating *seets* punctuated by several burbling warbles.

MIGRATE? Yes.

NESTING: Selects a high location in a conifer. Nest is hung from—or rests atop—a fork of branches, and is constructed with mosses and pieces of bark. Spider webbing is used for binding and anchoring. About 3 in. wide.

EGGS: Dull white. Length of ½ in. Total of 4-11, with 2 broods.

FEEDER BEHAVIOR: Does not visit feeders.

COMPARE TO SIMILAR SPECIES: Most similar to the closely related Ruby-crowned Kinglet, which lacks a striped face and a visible golden-yellow head crest.

DID YOU KNOW? The Golden-crowned Kinglet maintains an average internal body temperature of about 111 °F, which is 5-6 °F higher than that of most birds. Astonishingly, it is still able to survive long, cold winters at the northern extent of its breeding range: feasting on dormant caterpillars and insectile egg clusters by day, and roosting in sheltered crannies of trees by night.

J F M A M J J A S O N D

Adults at top and bottom.

Adult male at top (Note: Red throat may appear blackish from a more severe angle),
Adult female at bottom.

④ RUBY-THROATED HUMMINGBIRD.
Archilochus colubris.

SIZE: 3 ¼ in.

HABITAT: Edges of woods, overgrown fields, gardens, suburbs.

WILD DIET: Nectar from flowers, flying insects. Also, sugar water from feeders.

BEHAVIOR: This high-revving species feeds on flower nectar all throughout the day, supplemented by a trickle of protein-rich, flying insects. Hovering and precise flight are facilitated by a wing mechanism unique to the hummingbird family: unlike other birds, which fold the wings on the upstroke, this species is able rotate its shoulders to provide propulsive thrust in all directions throughout a single wingbeat. Also like most hummingbirds, this species must feed every 15 minutes during the day to meet its exorbitant energy demands; during the nighttime, it compensates by entering a state of partial hibernation, known as *torpor*.

MIGRATE? Yes.

NESTING: Selects a location on top of a deciduous tree branch. Cup-shaped mound is formed of spider silk, pollen, and mosses. About 2 in. across.

EGGS: White. Length of ½ in. Total of 2. Raises 1-2 broods each year, occasionally 3.

BIRD FEEDING TIPS

FEEDER DIET: Sugar water. **FEEDER TYPES**: Nectar feeders. **FEEDER BEHAVIOR**: Perches or hovers at feeders. Males may act territorially near single-feeder setups.

COMPARE TO SIMILAR SPECIES: Males are quite distinctive across the region. Females of this species are very similar to female Black-chinned Hummingbirds, which normally summer in Texas and farther west; note that the female Ruby-throated's folded wingtips are straight and much slimmer.

DID YOU KNOW? Before migrating across the Gulf of Mexico, millions of hummingbirds gather along the coast, doubling their weights in the several days immediately preceding their departure. This ocean crossing is grueling, with up to one-quarter of all migrants failing to complete the perilous journey.

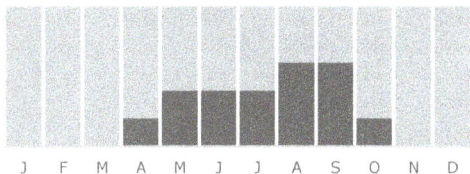

J F M A M J J A S O N D

INDEX OF SPECIES

SELECTED TITLES BY MARC PARNELL

The Birding Pro's Field Guides: City Series

Birds of Greater Chicago
Birds of Greater Cleveland, Pittsburgh, and Buffalo
Birds of Greater Dallas
Birds of Greater Houston
Birds of Greater New York City
Birds of Greater Washington, D.C.

The Birding Pro's Field Guides: State Series

Birds of Alabama
Birds of Arkansas
Birds of Connecticut
Birds of Delaware
Birds of Florida
Birds of Georgia
Birds of Iowa
Birds of Illinois
Birds of Indiana
Birds of Kansas
Birds of Kentucky
Birds of Louisiana
Birds of Massachusetts
Birds of Maryland
Birds of Michigan
Birds of Minnesota
Birds of Missouri

Birds of Mississippi
Birds of North Carolina
Birds of Nebraska
Birds of New Hampshire
Birds of New Jersey
Birds of New York
Birds of Ohio
Birds of Oklahoma
Birds of Pennsylvania
Birds of Rhode Island
Birds of South Carolina
Birds of Tennessee
Birds of Texas
Birds of Virginia
Birds of Vermont
Birds of Wisconsin
Birds of West Virginia

The Birding Pro's Field Guides: Province Series

Birds of Ontario

For a complete, updated list of titles, please visit our website at
www.thebirdingpro.com.

MARC PARNELL is a lifelong naturalist with a ceaseless passion for birding. He is currently the second most published ornithologist in the world by number of books in active print. Marc was born in Greenville, North Carolina, and presently resides in Cleveland, Ohio.

For press inquiries or event bookings, please contact the staff at Naturalist & Traveler Press, available at thebirdingpro.com.

If you enjoyed this field guide, please consider leaving a positive rating online at your place of purchase. As an independent publishing house, every bit of support is greatly appreciated.

Front Cover Photo: Ruby-throated Hummingbird
Back Cover Photos: American Kestrel, White-breasted Nuthatch